Switching
to Microsoft®
Windows 7

The Painless Way to Upgrade
From Windows XP or Vista

800 East 96th Street,
Indianapolis, Indiana 46240 USA

Switching to Microsoft® Windows 7: The Painless Way to Upgrade from Windows XP or Vista

Copyright © 2010 by Pearson Education, Inc.

ISBN-13: 978-0-7897-4221-6
ISBN-10: 0-7897-4221-7

Library of Congress Cataloging-in-Publication Data:

Tymes, Elna.

  Switching to Microsoft Windows 7 : the painless way to upgrade from Windows XP or Vista / Elna Tymes and Charles Prael.

   p. cm.

  ISBN 978-0-7897-4221-6

  1. Microsoft Windows (Computer file) 2. Operating systems (Computers) I. Prael, Charles E. II. Title.

  QA76.76.O63T945 2010

  005.4'46—dc22

                                        2009043154

Printed in the United States of America

First Printing: November 2009

Trademarks

All terms mentioned in this book that are known to be trademarks or service marks have been appropriately capitalized. Que Publishing cannot attest to the accuracy of this information. Use of a term in this book should not be regarded as affecting the validity of any trademark or service mark.

Warning and Disclaimer

Every effort has been made to make this book as complete and as accurate as possible, but no warranty or fitness is implied. The information provided is on an "as is" basis. The authors and the publisher shall have neither liability nor responsibility to any person or entity with respect to any loss or damages arising from the information contained in this book.

Bulk Sales

Que Publishing offers excellent discounts on this book when ordered in quantity for bulk purchases or special sales. For more information, please contact

> U.S. Corporate and Government Sales
> 1-800-382-3419
> corpsales@pearsontechgroup.com

For sales outside the United States, please contact

> International Sales
> international@pearson.com

Associate Publisher
Greg Wiegand

Acquisitions Editor
Rick Kughen

Development Editor
Rick Kughen

Managing Editor
Patrick Kanouse

Project Editor
Mandie Frank

Copy Editor
Barbara Hacha

Indexer
Tim Wright

Proofreader
Megan Wade

Technical Editor
Ron Barrett

Reviewers
Sean Carruthers
Todd Meister
Terri Stratton

Publishing Coordinator
Cindy Teeters

Book Designer
Anne Jones

Compositor
TnT Design, Inc.

Contents at a Glance

Table of Contents

About the Authors

Elna R. Tymes and **Charles E. Prael** are a writing team who have been authoring books about computers and software since the mid-1980s. They have written a large number of books and manuals about both Windows and Macintosh environments and have an active consulting practice working with Silicon Valley companies in the areas of program development, writing, and training. Working with their company, Los Trancos Systems, Tymes and Prael have developed a video server for Stanford University; standalone training material for Oracle and other Silicon Valley companies; and documentation sets for such widely diverse companies as Genentech, Apple, Sun Microsystems, and a host of smaller companies.

Dedication

To Adrian and Kelly: Thanks for dinners, backrubs, sufferance, and listening. There is room in our lives for flowers, sunshine, and cats.

Acknowledgments

This book would not have existed without the dedicated work of our agent, Carole Jelen of Waterside Productions. Finding new books to write at a time when the publishing industry is retrenching is difficult work.

We also want to thank our designated "naïve user," Al McCoy, for reading through the manuscript and pointing out things he didn't understand. If he couldn't figure it out, we rewrote it.

Thanks to all those bloggers who tirelessly dissect every new Microsoft release and point out features and problems. Staying on top of a not-quite-released product is easier because of you.

We Want to Hear from You!

As the reader of this book, *you* are our most important critic and commentator. We value your opinion and want to know what we're doing right, what we could do better, what areas you'd like to see us publish in, and any other words of wisdom you're willing to pass our way.

As an associate publisher for Que Publishing, I welcome your comments. You can email or write me directly to let me know what you did or didn't like about this book—as well as what we can do to make our books better.

Please note that I cannot help you with technical problems related to the topic of this book. We do have a User Services group, however, where I will forward specific technical questions related to the book.

When you write, please be sure to include this book's title and authors as well as your name, email address, and phone number. I will carefully review your comments and share them with the author and editors who worked on the book.

Email: feedback@quepublishing.com

Mail: Greg Wiegand
           Associate Publisher
           Que Publishing
           800 East 96th Street
           Indianapolis, IN 46240 USA

Reader Services

Visit our website and register this book at informit.com/register for convenient access to any updates, downloads, or errata that might be available for this book.

Introduction

What This Book Is About

This book is a guide to upgrading your computer operating system from Windows XP or from Windows Vista to Windows 7. It is intended to provide step-by-step instructions for planning your upgrade, dealing with application issues, exploring whether you should implement a virtual hard disk environment, and managing network issues.

So why do you need a book like this? Because we (the authors) have been through the process of upgrading our systems, both from Windows XP and Windows Vista, to Windows 7. We've made the mistakes and gotten in trouble and had to start over, but most importantly we've learned from our mistakes and used that experience to help us write this book. We've tested everything we've written here and revised some procedures as we encountered problems. The result is steps and procedures that work.

Probably the most important thing we did is figure out what we needed to know before we started. Nothing makes you want to tear out some hair like realizing that your hard disk is too full to allow you to install a new system while you're in mid-setup. The forms we show in the first few chapters were developed as we were migrating our own systems and reflect what we found we should have had on hand before beginning.

Among the problems we encountered were the older applications we'd been comfortably using for years that suddenly didn't work under Windows 7, or worked differently. So we've devoted a couple of chapters to looking at the impact of upgrading your system on those comfy ways you used to get your work done.

The good part about Windows 7 is that it works the way you'd expect an operating system to work. Chief among its valuable features is that it seems to be quite stable, unlike its predecessor Vista. In our five months of running Windows 7, it never crashed on us. So while we can't promise that you won't have any problems running Windows 7, we can say that you should expect a much more reliable operating environment.

This book is not intended to serve as a reference manual with explanations of all the new features and commands, nor is it intended to serve as a user guide for those who are new to Windows operating systems. Other books on the market address these areas.

However, this book will lead you through the process of analyzing your existing environment, installing the new Windows 7 software, and tailoring it to your computing environment, whether that's a personal laptop, a home computer, or a networked office computing system. One chapter ("New Windows 7 Features") briefly covers some of the new, key features in Windows 7. Chapter 7, "New Windows 7 Applications," discusses some of the major new applications available under Windows 7. And we haven't forgotten about networking (including wireless networking) and security issues—chapters 8-10 are devoted to those subjects. And we've covered how to use Windows 7 to virtually run other systems, too—such as running a Linux environment under Windows 7 in Chapter 11, "Virtualization."

Who Should Read This Book?

We have aimed this book at the reasonably proficient computer user—someone who is responsible for the hardware and software on his or her computer and has used at least one prior version of Windows. This user is not new to computers, and in particular to a Windows environment, but is familiar with the process of installing and upgrading hardware and software, although he or she probably needs checklists and reminders as the process unfolds. We're not expecting our readers to be full-time system administrators, although we believe that some of our readers will have that level of proficiency.

However, even those relatively new to system upgrades will be able to follow and apply the instructions we've provided in this book.

What This Book Will Do

When finished with this book, you will be able to do the following:

- Find and list your computer's internal memory, CPU size, internal and external hard disk space, existing operating system and level, and existing application programs.

- Make informed decisions about the use of one or more virtual hard disks.

- Analyze the impact of moving your applications and data from one Windows environment to Windows 7 before you actually do so.

- Successfully move applications from one Windows environment to Windows 7.

- Decide about new Windows 7 applications.

- Understand how your new Windows 7 computer will function in a networked environment.

- Upgrade your system from Windows XP to Windows 7.

- Upgrade your system from Windows Vista to Windows 7.

- Decide on and implement chosen applications new with Windows 7.

- Understand how to link a system to the Internet, to other networks, and to a wireless network.

- Understand the pros and cons of running Windows 7 or other operating systems in a virtual environment

If You're Upgrading from Windows XP

We have some bad news for you: you can't get directly to Windows 7 from Windows XP. Microsoft has made it impossible to upgrade directly, so unless you are loading Windows 7 on a new PC (one that doesn't have XP installed on it), you'll first have to acquire and install a copy of Windows Vista. Your Vista package doesn't have to be the fanciest, and in fact it will probably suit you better if it's the least-expensive version you can find. You will need the license number, however, and it will have to be legitimate or the Microsoft verification process will fail. The entire process is spelled out in Chapter 3, "Migrating from XP to Windows 7."

However, after you get to Windows Vista, the upgrade to Windows 7 should be relatively painless.

If You're Upgrading from Windows Vista

Migrating from Windows Vista to Windows 7 is fairly easy. We spell out the steps in Chapter 4, "Migrating from Vista to Windows 7." You'll find that fewer problems occur with Windows 7 than with Windows Vista. (At least that has been our experience.) You'll also find a lot of familiar aspects, features, and applications, although the Windows 7 user interface has been simplified and rewritten to make it more user friendly, and there are many new applications and new features.

Upgrading in a Networked Environment

Whether you're using a single computer hooked up to a printer and maybe some other peripheral devices (such as a scanner) at home, or you're a home-based worker who has to navigate corporate networks, you'll appreciate the ease of connecting to networks with Windows 7. New connectivity features in Windows 7 make it easy to identify what needs to be upgraded and what needs tailoring. Because Windows 7 is backward compatible with both Windows XP and Windows Vista, programs that run under those environments will still run under Windows 7. Programs running under even earlier versions of Windows are mostly compatible, too.

Getting Ready to Upgrade

One of the hardest parts of upgrading your system from one operating system level to another (or from one system to another) is knowing in advance what you'll need to know during the upgrade process. Frequently, the scripted steps ask you for a serial number or the name of a device or some other identifying information. Having tripped over this kind of problem ourselves, we decided to devote the first couple of chapters to getting you ready to move from one environment to another. We've provided some checklists that may seem tedious at first but ultimately will prove useful as you move through the upgrade process.

New Features and Applications

As could be expected, you'll find a number of new features and new applications with Windows 7. Some of these will be fairly attractive to most users; some may be attractive only to people working within a corporate network or to those who have to manage such a network. We haven't addressed every new feature or application, choosing to focus on those we think will have the widest appeal. You'll find these discussed in Chapters 6 and 7.

About Security

Microsoft takes computer security seriously and has made considerable improvements to various aspects of securing data on your system. Although some of the security provisions have been moved to related applications such as Internet Explorer 8.0, Windows 7 includes improvements to securing your data in both a home or small office networked environment and in an environment in which there are multiple users of one computer. Further, Windows 7 provides security advancements when hooking up your computer to external networks, whether those are the casual wireless networks available at a local coffee shop or the big networks sometimes used by business consultants. We look at security provisions in some detail in Chapter 8, "Windows 7 Security."

Networks and Windows 7

Most computers these days use a network, at least to share devices such as a printer or a scanner, but more often to access the Internet. Windows 7 has made it easy to identify, connect to, and use a variety of networks. Some of the networking screens have moved from where they were in Vista to a new part of Windows 7, and this may initially frustrate the new user. The screen you see when you first open Windows 7 should make it easy to find the networking features you're looking for. Chapters 9 and 10 discuss both networking with Windows 7 in general and wireless networking in particular.

A Word About Virtual Hard Disks

A virtual hard disk (VHD) is a single file containing a copy of an entire hard disk, including the operating system. This file can be replicated in other environments, such as a different hard disk, which can make backing up your system a breeze.

However, a lot of users find that they need to maintain working environments in several operating systems, such as Windows and UNIX or Linux, for instance. Windows 7 has two features to help you accomplish this: virtual hard disks, used in creating virtual systems, and the new Windows XP virtualization feature, called Windows XP Mode. The former makes it easy to create a copy of the disk where your copy of Windows 7 resides to, for example, a thumb drive so that the environment can be replicated on another machine (such as a laptop). Windows XP Mode lets you keep your Windows XP environment if, for instance, you don't want to upgrade some of the applications that were formerly running under Windows XP; it lets you run those applications the same as if you were still running Windows XP. Virtualization is covered in Chapter 11.

1

Planning Your Upgrade

Upgrading from one operating system to another is no longer as simple as inserting a diskette and pressing the Enter key. Questions arise about the right hardware, about compatibility of existing applications and data files with the new operating system, and about what effect the new operating system will have in a networked environment.

This chapter helps you analyze your existing environment and provides a checklist to help you think through the process of upgrading to Windows 7. It is not a comprehensive analysis—no book could cover all the variations in user environments—but it will cover the most common situations and applications.

Which Version of Windows 7?

Windows 7 has been released in six versions, each aimed at a different level of user. Although Microsoft expects that most users will choose either Windows 7 Home Premium for consumers or Windows 7 Professional for business users, this section helps you identify which of the six versions is appropriate for you. Microsoft says that it has made sure that all Windows 7 versions are compatible so that when customers upgrade from one version to the next, their files will work the same way as in a previous edition.

Windows 7 Starter Edition

Windows 7 Starter Edition is primarily for small-notebook users and those with limited-capacity computers, such as netbooks. This version is available only preinstalled on a computer by computer makers, such as Dell and HP. However, this version has some new user interfaces, such as a better task bar and Jump Lists, which allow you to get quickly from place to place, although it doesn't have the Aero Glass interface that lets you "look through" the panes of some windows to see the desktop. You'll be able to join a Home Group so you can share pictures, video, and audio files over a local network, and you'll be able to resolve problems through the Action Center and quickly back up and restore files.

Windows 7 Home Basic

Windows 7 Home Basic is available only in emerging markets around the world and is not available for sale in the United States. It has a 64-bit version as well as the 32-bit version, runs the equivalent of Vista's Media Center (which was included with higher-end versions of Vista), and lets you run unlimited applications at the same time. It has the Aero Glass interface, and Aero Peek gives you thumbnail previews when you move your cursor over the task bar. It has better network support, such as sharing an Internet connection (including via wireless) and power and network management for laptops.

Windows 7 Home Premium

Windows 7 Home Premium has all the visual enhancements of a full Windows 7 system, including all the major features of the Starter Edition and Home Basic versions. It provides touchscreen capability (for things such as handwriting recognition and multitouch) and has improved media format support over what was available in Vista, plus enhancements to the Windows Media Center and the capability to handle streaming media, DVD playback and creation, premium games, as well as the Mobility Center, where you can manage mobile options such as laptops, notebooks, and even cell phones.

Windows 7 Professional

Windows 7 Professional has more security and networking features, such as an encrypting file system, advanced network backup, and Domain Join—the capability to manage joined networks. Further, this version supports location-aware printing and advanced backup.

Windows 7 Enterprise and Windows 7 Ultimate

Windows 7 Enterprise and Windows 7 Ultimate are aimed more at corporate users and have advanced features such as data protection for internal and external hard drives through BitLocker, support for corporate networking based on Windows Server 2008 R2 (through Direct Access), the capability to prevent unauthorized software from running (AppLocker), and speeding up access to large remote files from branch offices (BranchCache).

Table 1.1 summarizes the differences between the versions of Windows 7.

Table 1.1 Windows 7 Features by Version

Version	Starter	Home Basic	Home Premium	Professional	Enterprise	Ultimate
Intended For	OEM Licensing	Emerging Markets	Retail and OEM Licensing	Retail and OEM Licensing	Volume Licensing	Retail and OEM Licensing
64-bit and 32-bit versions	32-bit only	Both	Both	Both	Both	Both
Maximum physical memory (64-bit only)	N/A	8GB	16GB	192GB	192GB	192GB
Home Group (create and join)	Join only	Join only	Yes	Yes	Yes	Yes
Multiple monitors	No	Yes	Yes	Yes	Yes	Yes
Fast user switching	No	Yes	Yes	Yes	Yes	Yes
Changeable desktop wallpaper	No	Yes	Yes	Yes	Yes	Yes
Desktop Window Manager	No	Yes	Yes	Yes	Yes	Yes
Windows Mobility Center	No	Yes	Yes	Yes	Yes	Yes
Windows Aero	No	Partial	Yes	Yes	Yes	Yes
Multitouch	No	No	Yes	Yes	Yes	Yes
Premium games included	No	No	Yes	Yes	Yes	Yes
Windows Media Center	No	No	Yes	Yes	Yes	Yes
Windows Media Player Remote Media Experience	No	No	Yes	Yes	Yes	Yes
Encrypting File System	No	No	No	Yes	Yes	Yes
Location Aware Printing	No	No	No	Yes	Yes	Yes

continues

Table 1.1   continued

Version	Starter	Home Basic	Home Premium	Professional	Enterprise	Ultimate
Intended For	OEM Licensing	Emerging Markets	Retail and OEM Licensing	Retail and OEM Licensing	Volume Licensing	Retail and OEM Licensing
Remote Desktop Host	No	No	No	Yes	Yes	Yes
Presentation Mode	No	No	No	Yes	Yes	Yes
Windows Server domain	No	No	No	Yes	Yes	Yes
Windows XP Mode	No	No	No	Yes	Yes	Yes
AppLocker	No	No	No	No	Yes	Yes
BitLocker Drive Encryption	No	No	No	No	Yes	Yes
BranchCache Distributed Cache	No	No	No	No	Yes	Yes
DirectAccess	No	No	No	No	Yes	Yes
Subsystem for UNIX-based Applications	No	No	No	No	Yes	Yes
Multilingual User Interface Pack	No	No	No	No	Yes	Yes
Virtual Hard Disk Booting	No	No	No	No	Yes	Yes

Hardware

Both Vista and XP used the Windows Hardware Compatibility List (for hardware) and Windows Logo'd Product List (for software) to ensure that your favorite devices and applications would work with those versions of Windows. With Windows 7, you can look at the Windows 7 Compatibility List window to see if your current hardware works with Windows 7 or whether you need a new driver. You can also look at the Logo'd Product List to determine whether you need a software upgrade.

Windows Compatibility List

The Windows 7 Upgrade Advisor is a Website that makes it easy for you to evaluate whether your system is compatible with Windows 7. It has links to the Upgrade Advisor program, advice on the process, links to downloadable versions of Windows 7, and information about system requirements. To download the Upgrade Advisor, visit the following Microsoft Website at http://www.microsoft.com/windows/windows-7/get/upgrade-advisor.aspx.

Generally, if your computer can run Windows Vista, it can run Windows 7. However, if you're not running Windows Vista or are unsure whether your system can run Windows 7, here's how to check.

1. Before you run the Windows 7 Upgrade Advisor Beta, be sure to plug in any USB devices or other devices such as printers, external hard drives, or scanners that are regularly used with the computer you're evaluating. They are needed for the evaluation.

2. Download, install, and run the Windows 7 Upgrade Advisor Beta.

3. You'll get a report on whether your PC can run Windows 7 and if there are any known compatibility issues.

4. If an issue can't be easily resolved, you'll get suggestions for next steps. For example, it might let you know that you need an updated driver for your printer and where to get it. Or the suggestions might include a recommendation that you buy a newer computer to fully experience features of Windows 7.

Windows Logo'd Products

Programs that have earned the "Certified for Windows 7" logo or the "Works with Windows 7" logo are officially supported on Windows 7 by Microsoft's independent software vendor (ISV) partners. The "Certified for Windows 7" logo identifies products that are designed and tested to deliver a superior experience with Windows 7. The "Works with Windows 7" logo lets you know which software and devices offer baseline compatibility with Windows 7. To find which products are compatible with Windows 7, use a search engine to find references to "Windows 7 Logo'd Products." If you do this search shortly after Windows 7 has been released, the updates to the relevant Microsoft sites may not have been posted.

Many programs are compatible and work well with Windows 7 but are not included in the websites. Some programs are not included because they have not yet gone through the Windows 7 logo program, or because they are still completing the program. New programs are continually being added to the program.

Hardware Checklist

Before you can know what you'll need to run Windows 7, you need to know what you already have. The following checklists will help you determine the capacity of your existing environment and what you also need to run Windows 7. Use Table 1.2 to determine if your hardware will run Windows 7:

Table 1.2   Minimum Requirements for Windows 7 (All Editions)

Have?	Description	Minimum	Notes
	Main processor 32 bit (x86) or 64-bit (X64)	1GHz	When you start your computer after it has been turned off, your operating system checks for processor size and type. Watch carefully as the data scrolls by on your screen, but you should see this information before Windows starts.
	System memory	1GB RAM	This number will also appear as the data scrolls by.
	Internal hard disk	16GB for 32-bit processors; 20GB for 64-bit processors	This is the disk usually referred to as Drive C:. You may have to use a Windows utility to find how much space is available.
	DirectX 9 graphics device with WDDM 1.0 or later driver		See the "Graphics Support" section later in this chapter.
	DVD-ROM drive		See the "DVD Drive" section later in this chapter.
	Audio output		Speakers are usually built in to a laptop computer and are frequently included when you buy a desktop system.
	Internet access	DSL, cable, or other high-speed access	Usually enabled with a browser.

Multicores Versus Multi-CPUs

Although all editions of Windows 7 can support multicore CPUs, only Windows 7 Professional, Ultimate, and Enterprise can support multiple CPUs. The difference is a small but important one. Multiple CPUs refers to having more than one CPU chip on a single motherboard. Multiple-CPU systems are generally used in environments in which a great deal of computing capability is needed that fits in a small physical space—data centers, animation rendering farms, and other such places.

Multiple cores, on the other hand, refer to having more than one CPU core on a single chip. This was introduced in 2005 as a means of providing more computational capability on a single CPU chip. Most commercial desktop and laptop systems these days are offered with multiple cores, although they still come with only a single actual CPU chip.

More Than the Minimum

Beyond what Microsoft considers the minimum hardware required to run the operating system, you should also consider what equipment would make your system work the best. We're not recommending you upgrade your hardware to the point where it resembles a supercomputer. However, at some places you will want to have more than the minimum.

Following are the key things you need to consider from a hardware perspective before upgrading to Windows 7.

CPU

The more powerful your central processor, the faster your computer will perform its operations, up to a point. A lot of users keep more than one application open at a time, allowing for an application, such as a browser, to continually download email as it arrives. Other users play music or listen to the radio as a background task while working on some other application, such as a word processing document or a spreadsheet. Having more than one application running at the same time uses both processor cycles and memory.

Further, some applications run more slowly when the CPU has less power. Having a fast CPU allows for faster updating of complex spreadsheet calculations, large graphics, or continually updated Websites.

Memory

Another big problem is trying to run applications in too little memory (RAM). When an application opens, it needs both CPU cycle time and working memory space in RAM. When you open a document, for instance, the application copies a portion of the file from the disk space where it has been stored into working memory space, with an index as to where the rest of the file is stored. As you enter your changes or add new information to the portion in working memory, the application keeps both the previous version of the file and the new version in working memory, until you save the file (or the program automatically saves it for you). The longer you work without saving your corrections, the more memory is needed for both versions of your file. This can get particularly hazardous if you are inserting or deleting large chunks of information. If you run out of memory, you may lose portions of your new file.

When you approach the limit of your system's internal memory, Windows uses swap space (virtual memory, which is actually space on a hard disk). Although this solves the immediate memory requirement, it also causes an enormous performance problem: access to any data stored on the hard disk (in this case, the swap space) takes between 100 and 1,000 times longer than access to data stored in RAM.

How much memory you should have is up to you. Given the memory requirements of most application programs today, and given that the cost of memory has been coming down steadily over the past two decades, it makes sense to have at least 1GB of internal memory, and more if you think you'll need it.

Table 1.3 provides some guidelines for the type of applications commonly run on today's computers and their typical memory usage. Remember, you'll definitely want to run more than one application at a time (possibly as many as five or more) so plan your memory allowance accordingly.

Table 1.3   Recommended RAM for Selected Applications

Application Type	Average RAM Usage
Base system memory (memory needed by Windows to operate)	1GB
Office productivity software	500MB
Local email storage	250MB
Graphics editing, such as Photoshop	Anywhere from 250MB to 2GB, depending on the resolution of the pictures you will be editing
Audio editing	500MB
Video editing	1–2GB
Accounting software	250–500MB
Gaming	Varies tremendously, but more memory will improve game play, particularly if you play graphics-intensive games

To determine how much you'll need, add the amounts required for a reasonable combination of software packages that you'll be running at the same time. If, for example, you plan to do some photo and video editing and use your computer for normal office work (email, letters, spreadsheets), it's unlikely that you'll be using your word processing software at the same time you edit your pictures. However, if you're assembling a newsletter that contains pictures, you may need to edit your pictures to fit into your newsletter, meaning that you'll need both applications to be open simultaneously. So the smart thing is to have the memory available to run both packages at the same time.

tip

Given the numbers shown in Table 1.3, we'd suggest 1GB for the operating system, plus 500MB for the office productivity software, plus at least 1GB for picture editing—for a total of at least 2.5GB of RAM.

However, memory is one of the cheapest system performance upgrades you can get. Memory is relatively inexpensive—on the order of $30–$50/GB. Adding or upgrading your system memory is thus a simple, low-cost operation, if you know what you're doing. If you have doubts about your abilities, find a local computer technician for whom it should be a quick, simple operation.

There is an upper limit on the amount of memory you can install. The 32-bit version of Windows 7 (running on x86/Pentium/Athlon computers) has an absolute upper limit of 3GB of physically addressable memory. For reference, the 64-bit (x64) version of Windows 7 can address an effectively unlimited amount of memory (the actual limit is 2^64 bytes, or 16 exabytes, which as of December 2008 was more RAM than had ever been made). In practice, the 64-bit limit is 192GB of memory. The exact amount of usable memory will differ, depending on which version of Windows 7 you install, as shown in Table 1.4.

Table 1.4   Usable Memory, Windows 7 Versions

Version	Architecture	Addressable Memory
Any Windows 7 version	32-bit	3.37GB
Windows 7 Start, Home Basic	64-bit	8GB
Windows 7 Home Premium	64-bit	16GB
Windows 7 Professional, Enterprise, Ultimate	64-bit	192GB

tip

If you plan to run only Windows 7 on your computer, any memory beyond that upper limit may not be useful. However, you should note that the latest versions of Linux have no problem making use of 4GB+ of memory. If you plan to use a dual-boot or virtual system (with Windows 7 running in a virtual environment, inside a Linux OS), putting 4GB or more of memory into your system is probably a good idea.

note

So what's the difference between a 32-bit system and a 64-bit system? In your computer, the data bus connects memory to the rest of the system, including the processor, and moves the data around inside your computer. In a 32-bit computer, the width (or size) of the data bus is 32 bits. A 64-bit bus is twice as wide so the system can move twice as much data around. Being able to process more data in a single operation usually means a faster system. Normal office applications and web surfing will not show any noticeably faster progress with a 64-bit system, but graphics processing and scientific calculations will run much faster.

Disk Space

As we noted earlier in this chapter, Windows 7 requires a minimum of 15GB of available disk space and requires at least a 20–40GB hard disk, depending on which version of Windows 7 you are installing. This extra space allows for some data storage, provides free disk space for swap space (as discussed previously), and allows you to download web pages and possibly run a few programs.

However, disk space is so inexpensive these days that if 20–40GB of disk space is all that you have available, you may want to either upgrade your existing hard disk or get some more external storage.

Unless your office environment requires that you store all your data files on networked drives, we recommend that you have at least a 40GB disk drive. If your current system is on a much smaller hard disk, you should look at Chapters 3 and 4 for information on how to migrate your system while doing a hard disk upgrade. If your system is new, it's likely that it came with 100 or more gigabytes of disk space (and some systems are shipping with a whopping terabyte or more of disk storage space).

Graphics Support

Windows 7 Basic needs support for DirectX 9 graphics and 32MB of graphics memory. Windows 7 Premium needs support for DirectX 9 graphics with a WDDM driver, at least 128MB of graphics memory, Pixel Shader 2.0 (hardware), and a graphics resolution of 32 bits per pixel.

DirectX is Microsoft's Applications Program Interface model within the operating system between the applications (games, programs, and the like) and the video hardware. DirectX 9 graphic support means that the video card (or chip, if your video is built in on your motherboard) must provide support for DirectX v9 graphics APIs. DirectX 8 was the first version released on Windows XP, and subsequently it bumped to DirectX 9. DirectX 10 is exclusive to Windows Vista and isn't supported on Windows XP.

To check for which version of DirectX you have

1. Click the Start button and choose the Run option.

2. Enter **dxdiag** and click Run.

3. Click OK in the check box to allow dxdiag to examine your system. The DirectX Diagnostic Tool appears (as shown in Figure 1.1). Among the other information that the system collects about your system is the DirectX version, which you can check by looking at the bottom of the System tab.

4. Click Exit to close the dxdiag tool.

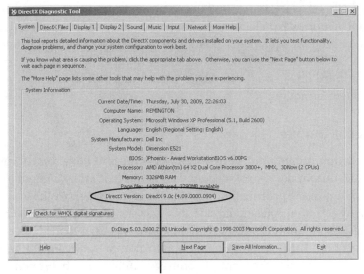

The version of DirectX that is installed on your system is shown here. You need a minimum of DirectX 9.0 to run Windows 7.

FIGURE 1.1

Use the DirectX Diagnostic Tool to make sure that your version of DirectX will work with Windows 7.

The easiest way to ensure that your existing system is up-to-date with DirectX 9 is to run full system updates from the Microsoft update Website at http://update.microsoft.com/windowsupdate/, including optional updates, and make sure that the system updates include DirectX 9.

Under Windows 7, you can enable Aero and play videos reasonably well using an AGP graphics card with 128MB or more VRAM. Choose your graphics card from those listed on the Windows 7 Compatibility List.

DVD Drive

The difference between a CD-ROM drive and a DVD-ROM drive is largely one of capacity: a CD has considerably less storage space than does a DVD, and Windows 7 takes up about 2GB of storage.

By far, the majority of Windows 7 users will receive a DVD containing Windows 7 when they purchase the package and will need a DVD-ROM drive to install the software. (Some corporate users will install from an image, which gets converted to DVD.) But you should back up your new software on some form of external disk, either an external hard disk or a DVD-ROM. That way, if something happens to your executable form of

Windows 7, you can reinstall the software. If you purchase a computer with Windows 7 preloaded, the computer manufacturer (often referred to as an original equipment manufacturer, or OEM) will include a restore disk or include the Windows 7 installation files in a separate partition on your hard drive. See the documentation that came with your computer for more information.

Audio Output

Although not mandatory, it's a very good idea to have some form of audio output device installed on your computer. Many computers come with a pair of speakers that plug into your computer. At the very least, many programs give audio signals when errors occur. Windows has a musical signal that indicates the program has been loaded after being turned off. Further, some of your application programs might provide sound effects, whether that's in games, surfing the web, listening to the radio, or watching videos.

Internet Access

Because you're planning to install Windows 7, you'll need access to the Internet—to verify the license key if nothing else. In addition, some support functions and other features require Internet access. You can use any browser that is compatible with your current operating system, but after you've installed Windows 7, you should verify that the browser is designed to work with Windows 7.

The single biggest reason you'll need Internet access is to register your new Windows 7 software with Microsoft. Without that registration being complete, you won't be using an authorized copy.

We've tested Internet access under Internet Explorer and found that Internet access basically works the same way as under Windows XP and Windows Vista. However, the way you connect to the Internet now involves a new set of steps. These are explained in more detail in Chapter 9, "Windows Networking."

note

You may use other browsers, such as Mozilla Firefox, Apple's Safari, or Google's Chrome. See the documentation with those browsers for additional details.

Finding Out What You Have

When you install a new operating system, your existing software doesn't go away (unless you reformat the drive as part of the installation process). Depending on what portions of Windows 7 you choose to install, you may find that some of your application programs may not work as well as they did before, or may not, in fact, work at all.

Before you install any portion of Windows 7, look at the System Information windows:

1. For Vista users, click the Start button at the bottom of your screen, select Control Panel, and then select System. Here, you can see basic information about your computer (see Figure 1.2).

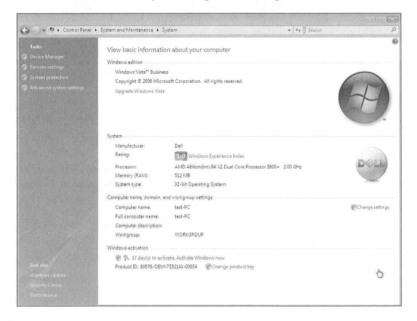

FIGURE 1.2

The Vista System window shows basic information about your computer, such as the version of Windows running, installed memory, and so on.

2. For XP users, click the Start button at the bottom of your screen, select the Control Panel, then select System, and choose the General tab (see Figure 1.3).

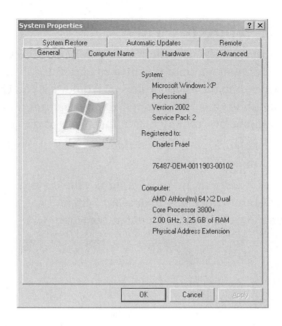

FIGURE 1.3

In XP, you can see your version of Windows by looking at the General tab on the System Control Panel.

3. Find and note on a piece of paper your existing operating system and Service Pack level (assuming that you have installed service packs via Windows Update).

4. To determine what applications you have installed, click the My Computer icon, click Drive C:, and open the Program Files folder (as shown in Figure 1.4).

5. For each application, list the program name and version on the same piece of paper on which you noted the existing operating system information.

FIGURE 1.4

Program Files installed on this computer.

Back Up, Back Up, Back Up!

Face it: you need to back up your data. And doing it while you're in the planning stage means that you won't forget it later, when things could get confusing. Most important are the data files on Drive C: (particularly those stored in the Documents and Settings folder and those stored in the MS Office folder) or the data files stored directly on your desktop. Use the Backup utility in your Windows software to efficiently back up your data files, but be sure to back them up onto something external to your desktop system (such as a DVD-ROM or an external hard disk).

Backing Up Under Windows Vista

Depending on your version of Windows Vista, you can use either the Automatic Backup to back up just your files and data or the Complete PC Backup to back up everything on your PC, including the operating system and applications.

To back up your files, follow these steps:

1. Click the Start button and select Control Panel.

2. Click System Maintenance and select Back Up Your Computer.

3. Click either the Back Up Files button or the Back Up Computer button. Vista will ask you where you want the backup file stored. Specify a drive (hard drive or USB thumb drive) that is different from the one on which your files are stored.

caution

If you choose Back Up Files, you should include the data files that you want to back up. These can include documents, music, pictures, email, Favorites, saved games, cookies, registration information for software you purchase and/or registered online, iTunes playlists, and so on. The whole point of a backup operation is to make sure that you have a duplicate version of files you want to keep, stored in an area that won't be affected if your system crashes or a hard drive fails or some other calamity happens. If you are unsure how to save (or locate) things such as your email or saved playlists, open each application and search the Help menu or search online for steps. Do this BEFORE you start the backup process to ensure that you know where everything is and that you haven't left anything out.

4. Then click the Start Backup button. Vista will proceed to create either a backup image of all your files and folders or a complete image of your computer, including the operating system and applications, depending on your choice.

Backing Up Under Windows XP

If you use Windows XP Professional, you can use the built-in Backup utility to help you make copies of files, settings, or everything on your computer. You can even use the utility to back up certain files on a schedule that you specify.

note

See the Caution under "Backing Up under Windows Vista" earlier in this chapter for tips on which data files to back up, as well as system and program files.

1. Click Start, and select All Programs.

2. Select Accessories, and then click System Tools.

3. Click Backup.

4. You'll see the Backup or Restore Wizard welcome window (see Figure 1.5). Click Next and follow the instructions on the wizard.

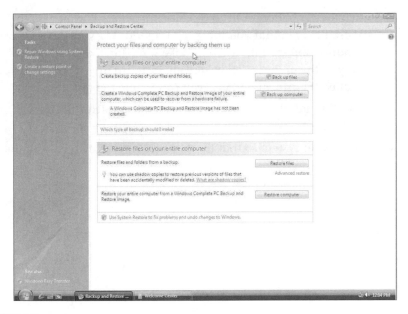

FIGURE 1.5

Backup and Restore Center in Vista.

Running Windows Update

Regardless of which version of Windows you've been running, when you get ready to upgrade to Windows 7, you need to be sure that you're working with software that has been updated recently. Some older versions of both Windows XP and Windows Vista may not provide a clear upgrade path without recent patches being installed before you start the upgrade to Windows 7.

To determine whether your current Windows system has been updated, follow these steps:

1. Go to www.Microsoft.com.

2. Click the Security & Updates tab.

3. Select the Security Home page.

4. On the Security window, scroll down to the Search by Product/Technology and Service Pack window.

5. Enter the product for which you want to check for updates, leave the Service Pack item set to All, click all the Update Severity Rating boxes, and leave the Bulletin Release Date box set to All.

6. Click the Go button. A list of updates appears, allowing you to choose the ones that you think are important to your system's performance and security. This can take some time, depending on how many of the updates you've already installed. If you have already installed the critical updates, you can ignore the rest.

7. Work through this list until you've installed at least the critical updates.

8. Reboot your system so that the new updates are merged with the older software.

2

Applications

Now that you've decided what to do about your hardware and your operating system software, you need to deal with the programs where you likely spend most of your computer time: the application programs. These can include such things as your Internet browser, your word processing package, the games you play (in your spare time, of course), the programs you use for database access and analysis, and so on.

Evaluating Applications for Upgrading or Cross-Grading

Many people use the occasion of a system upgrade as an opportunity to evaluate the applications on their systems. They're looking to determine whether they would benefit more by upgrading an existing application to a newer version or by cross-grading (transitioning to a different, better software package).

For instance, many people use the word processing, spreadsheet, and presentation packages (for example, Word, Excel, and PowerPoint) available as part of software suites, such as Microsoft Office. Because you're going to be upgrading your operating system, does it make sense to also upgrade your Office package to a more recent version?

Or perhaps your small business has been using an older version of SeaMonkey, a browser package, but you've found it inconvenient to deal with Websites that aren't compatible with it. Because you're going to change the operating system, maybe it's time to look at other browser alternatives and determine which browser and email solution makes the most sense for your current needs.

Perhaps, over time, people in your organization have upgraded to different versions of various applications to do the same thing, such as using different office productivity packages or different security software, each with different capabilities and different licenses. To ease support problems in the future, perhaps you'd like to standardize on a select group of applications, and because you're going to be changing the operating systems, now would be a good time to do so.

The only systematic way to do this is to list the applications under consideration and determine whether upgrading will cause compatibility issues: Can you open and edit files created under an older version of Word with a newer version of the same package? Can you still share files with others without causing compatibility issues? The same questions need to be answered if you're considering cross-grading: What happens to the old files created under a different application? Can the new software open these files? Will the old files be lost if you do, and if so, is that going to be a problem? How do you migrate profile information from one application to another?

You can efficiently answer these and other questions by doing a package-by-package evaluation, noting concerns that are important to your personal or office operation. Table 2.1 is a form you can use to evaluate your current and future applications needs.

Some packages have common capabilities from version to version, and an upgrade from one version to another won't cause compatibility problems. For instance, MS Word and Excel are backward compatible, meaning that documents and files created in a more recent version of the package can read files created in previous versions. However, problems can occur when you use a previous version of the package to open a file created under a newer version.

This is most likely to happen where you are transferring files between computers that are running different versions of the operating system, such as between a laptop and a desktop machine, or between your own computer and that of a client. One solution in Word, for instance, is to save the more current file in Rich Text Format (RTF) and then open it under the older software. Other file formats are visible in Word when you choose Save As from the File menu and scroll through the file format options in the drop-down box.

Another way around incompatibility issues is to use a viewer that some manufacturers provide. Microsoft, for instance, provides viewers that let you see files created in Office applications even if you don't have Office installed on your computer. This can be useful if you don't use Word but are trying to read a Word document sent by someone else.

Word, Excel, and PowerPoint viewers can be found by searching for the particular viewer at http://www.microsoft.com/downloads/en/default.aspx.

Table 2.1   Application Software Evaluation Form

Existing Package Name	Version #	Replacement Package Name	Version #	Pluses	Minuses	Purpose
MS Office	Office Pro 2003 Office 2000	MS Office	Office Pro Plus 2007	Widely used, some known problems, many new features, wide file-format compatibility, integration between apps. New user interface is slick.	Startup time for new users, backward compatibility issues, cost. New version of Office due next year. Licensing costs vs. open source. New user interface takes time to learn.	Office productivity software

We've filled in one package (MS Office Pro) to give you an idea of the items you should consider.

List the packages being considered for replacement in the first column and their version numbers in the second column. In the third column, list the packages being considered as replacements, along with their version numbers in the fourth column.

On a separate page, list attributes you want to compare. Summarize the results in the Pluses and Minuses columns. (You can see a comparison of three versions of Microsoft Word at www.microsoft.com/officebusiness/ products/compare-suites.aspx.)

This form is useful when talking about budgets. It helps make an argument for or against particular packages in functional terms, rather than being simply a request for new and better toys. It also helps you evaluate purchased software applications versus their open-source competitors.

A Word About Data Files

The other major consideration in upgrading or cross-grading is the data files. With your existing applications, most users have developed designated file areas where data files can be stored. For example, most people store their work in their My Documents folder. In corporate environments, in contrast, separate file areas and network storage locations may be used, to allow easier sharing and backup of shared data files. Other applications may, by default, store their data directly in the folder that the application was installed to.

Another related problem that often crops up is when changes to the software from one version to another have changed default locations or changed file types. A good example can be seen in office productivity software. Microsoft has, in roughly every other version, upgraded the file format used in Word, which means that every other version becomes somewhat incompatible with previous versions of Word. Similarly, open-source equivalents use similar-but-not-quite-the-same file formats.

To illustrate the problem more concretely, suppose you have a situation where one person with whom you swap files uses OpenOffice 2.1, another uses MS Office 2000, and a third uses MS Office 2007. The result is that the person using Office 2000 can see the files generated by the person using Open Office, but only with formatting problems, and he can't see the files created by the person using Office 2007 at all. Although this doesn't happen often in upgrades, it's a more common problem when changing from one application to another. It's also one of the primary reasons we stress that offices should adopt software standards. Making sure that your co-workers or people with whom you regularly share files are using the same version of the same software completely removes that issue and allows you to present a common front to the outside world.

Applying Application Standards to Older Operating Systems

Many users have old application programs, such as games or special-purpose utilities that no longer run on current operating systems. Perhaps you have a label-generation program that worked very well under Windows 95. Perhaps you have a favorite game that was released when Windows 3.1 was current. However, these applications don't work under Windows Vista and might not work well under Windows 7. Fortunately, there are solutions.

One is to use Windows XP Mode. This is available only on the higher-end versions of Windows 7, but it includes a Windows XP virtual system that integrates directly with your Windows 7 system, allowing you to access your programs directly from the Start menu. For more information, see Chapter 11, "Virtualization."

Another solution, if you are using one of the Home versions of Windows 7, is to install a virtualization package on your computer and run any applications that aren't compatible with Windows 7 in a Windows XP installation on a separate partition. See Chapter 11 for a discussion of the

various virtualization packages and how to get started with them, and see
Chapter 3, "Migrating from XP to Windows 7," for information on how to
migrate your applications from your current Windows XP system to the
new virtual system.

Migrating Applications

Because this book is more about migrating from Windows XP or Windows
Vista to Windows 7, let's focus on tools available to help move your programs in those three environments. Fortunately, Windows Easy Transfer,
available as part of your Vista installation package, makes this relatively
easy. In addition to Windows Easy Transfer, which will migrate your
application settings and data, other options allow complete migration of
both applications and data as a single operation.

Windows Easy Transfer, which is available for free from Microsoft's website, allows you to migrate both application settings and data from your
XP system to a Windows 7 system. It even allows you to create a disk
repository with this information.

Windows Easy Transfer lets you identify the programs and related data
that you want to transfer and accomplish most of this migration work in
one set of actions. The easiest workaround in transferring application data
from Windows XP to a Windows 7 environment is to use Windows Easy
Transfer on the Windows 7 DVD to transfer XP documents and settings to
a backup location (such as a thumb drive or to another hard disk) and
then restore from this backup once the Windows 7 installation is complete.

Step-by-step instructions for using this utility program to move your applications from one environment to another are covered in Chapter 3.

However, you may want to move other application programs and data
one at a time, rather than as a group. You may want to rearrange where
you store some programs and data, for instance, or apply different security standards to some programs. Or you may have other special considerations, such as the capability to store your application migration data
offline while you get the new operating system configuration worked out.

Chapter 5, "Application Migration," includes a much more exhaustive
discussion of various methods of migration for your application settings,
data, and even applications from an older system to a new Windows 7
system. In addition to Windows Easy Transfer, we also examine SpearIt's
MoveMe software (formerly offered by LapLink), as well as a product
called PC Relocator that is the basis for Windows Easy Transfer. Both of
these applications allow you to migrate applications as well as settings

and data. We highly recommend reading this chapter before performing any migration.

Dealing with Applications Versus Data

Some application programs, such as your browser or your email program, have your profiles stored where the application program resides, not where you keep your data files. Your browser and email profiles, for instance, probably include your preferences for HTML or text messages, any custom signatures, where deleted messages should go, pointers to all your stored messages, your bookmarks, whether to set cookies, how to handle pop-up windows, your privacy preferences, and so on. These are stored with the program, not as data files, and need to be on the same disk (real or virtual). On the other hand, your stored email files are probably stored in a different place from your email application files, and you may want to use the upgrade as an occasion to do some housekeeping and delete some of those old messages.

Following are some points you should keep in mind:

- You can use Windows Easy Transfer to move both programs and all their associated data as a package, but before you get to that stage, make sure that the move will transfer everything you want moved.

- If you're using the move as an opportunity to upgrade from one version of an application to another (for example, moving from one version of Microsoft Office to another version), you should do two things:

  - Verify that the new application is compatible with the new operating system (some applications that worked with Windows XP or Windows Vista may not work under Windows 7). This information is usually available on the web page of the company that sells the application, although you may have to search a bit.

  - Verify that the new version of the application will be able to use the data files from the older version. It may be that utilities in Windows 7 that are referenced by the newer version of the application won't look in the right place for your moved data files. A good way to prevent problems like this is to use the same shared folders to store data on the old system and the new system. If these shared folders are physically located on a separate, networked hard drive, you won't have to move any data files; just use the same drive designation and folder name as before.

---

note

There's no substitute for prior planning. Before beginning a migration, create a plan that details what's on the original system, where it is going to wind up on the new system configuration, and how you are going to get from one to the other.

Migration Versus Reinstallation

Generally, we prefer to migrate a software package intact. At times, however, that may not be an option—or it may not be the preferred option.

Some software packages register a unique ID based on both the license key and the CPU ID (which is a unique serial number stored in your computer's CPU) or the system ID (which is a similar unique serial number based on your system's hardware configuration). If you migrate from one physical system to another, or significantly change the hardware configuration, the ID may change, as will the unique ID used by that software package. When this happens, you are forced to reinstall the software, or at the very least verify that the software is legitimate by inserting the installation disk so it can be verified. Fortunately, this doesn't happen often and shouldn't be a problem. It is nonetheless something you should be aware of as a potential issue when you think about migration.

In some cases, migration may not be your preferred option. Sometimes your application configuration may get cluttered, for lack of a better term. This happens when customizations and application tweaks build up over time. When this occurs, it is sometimes a better choice to reinstall the application, starting with a clean slate.

However, it's always better to migrate an application, if you can without losing data, before resorting to reinstallation.

Cross-Grading Applications

Suppose you've decided to use an openware package, such as OpenOffice, instead of Microsoft Office, and you want to use the operating system migration as the opportunity to make the change, thus minimizing downtime. How do you transition to the new packages? For some software packages, such as office productivity software, the general procedure to cross-grade from one application can be relatively simple:

1. Make sure you can get to your data files from the new application.

2. Reset any template files you might want in the new application.

3. Where necessary, reinstall any add-ons that you use.

---

note

Cross-grading is an industry term developed from the practice of moving across from one application to a similar one from a different source. Rather than an upgrade or a downgrade, the activity came to be called a *cross-grade*.

In some situations, however, cross-grading becomes a bit more complex, such as when your application creates a variety of user profile files that then need to be moved to the new application. Let's go back to the example we discussed earlier in this chapter in the section "Evaluating Applications for Upgrading or Cross-Grading," in which we discussed moving from Office 2003 to Office 2007.

---

note

In our example, we decided to bite the bullet and migrate from SeaMonkey to Thuderbird and Firefox (email and web browsing packages).

In this case, we're in luck because utilities are available, making it relatively easy to import the profile information we're concerned about.

When you move to Firefox, follow these steps:

1. Install the Firefox software.

2. On the File menu, click Import to import the SeaMonkey profiles that you use regularly.

When you move to Thunderbird, follow these steps:

1. Install the Thunderbird software.

2. On the Tools menu, click Import.

3. One at a time, use this procedure to import your email messages, your address book, and your settings.

---

note

There's a gotcha in this process: After you've moved the files, you can't go back. So be very sure you want to import the files into the new application.

3

Migrating from XP to Windows 7

One of the most looked-for features in Windows 7 is a software upgrade directly from Windows XP to Windows 7. The reasons are simple and straightforward: there are three times as many XP licenses out there as Vista licenses, and many large corporate customers have specifically asked for an XP upgrade capability. In this, we are disappointed, because although Microsoft will allow a license upgrade from Windows XP to Windows 7, no software upgrade exists—you must perform a clean installation of Windows 7 and migrate your data into the new OS installation.

In fact, if you try to perform an in-place upgrade, you'll see the error message shown in Figure 3.1.

tip

That's the official Microsoft story. However, while we were writing this book we ran across a solution that allows you to do in-place upgrades from Windows XP systems to Windows 7. This is possible using the newest version of LapLink's PC Mover software. For more information on this, see Chapter 5, "Application and Data Migration".

When migrating a system from Windows XP to Windows 7, you should use the following sequence of activities:

1. Run the Windows 7 Upgrade Advisor and determine any potential hardware issues.

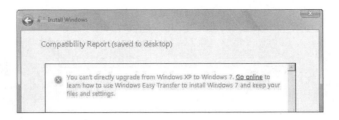

FIGURE 3.1

Attempting to upgrade from Windows XP to Windows 7 will result in a unwelcome error message.

> **tip**
>
> It is entirely possible that your computer running Windows XP lacks the minimum hardware requirements for running Windows 7. If that is the case, you're likely looking at purchasing a new PC with Windows 7 preloaded, building your own PC, and loading Windows 7 yourself or upgrading the hardware in your current XP computer and suffering through the arduous upgrade process described in this chapter.

2. Use a migration tool to snapshot your Windows XP system state, including all installed applications and data, and prepare for migration. We highly recommend Windows Easy Transfer.

3. Install Windows 7.

4. Resolve any driver issues within Windows 7.

5. Use your migration tool to install applications and data.

Before you attempt a Windows XP to Windows 7 migration, we strongly recommend that you read this entire chapter, as well as Chapter 8, "Windows 7 Security," make sure you have all the software and hardware tools you need at hand, and use the plan you created in Chapter 1, "Planning Your Migration," as a map to proceed. Over a number of years, we have found that well-planned migrations generally work out quite well, whereas ad-hoc migrations, where you jump right in, inevitably run into problems. Remember: Prior Planning Prevents Poor Performance.

Windows 7 Upgrade Advisor

Before upgrading a Windows XP system to Windows 7, you should first download the Microsoft Windows Upgrade Advisor from www.microsoft.com/windows/windows-7/upgrade-advisor.aspx.

Depending on how your browser is set up, you may directly run the installer or be prompted to save it. If you're dealing with only a single computer, it is a simple process. If, however, you're dealing with multiple computers, you should probably save it because you will need to install and run the upgrade advisor on each of the computers.

After you've downloaded it, install the Upgrade Advisor on the system you want to upgrade. Then run the Upgrade Advisor (see Figure 3.2).

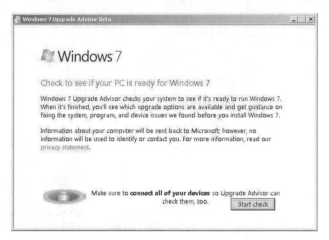

FIGURE 3.2

Windows 7 Upgrade Advisor Start screen.

Click the Start Check button, and let the Upgrade Advisor examine your system. It will look at your hardware configuration and compare it to a comprehensive database of supported hardware and software.

Depending on your specific system configuration, your system may pass on first examination, such as the system shown in Figure 3.3

However, you might run into issues that need to be resolved before you can install Windows 7, as shown in Figure 3.4.

In the example in Figure 3.4, the reason the system check failed was because the hardware necessary to run Windows Aero wasn't available. You can still run Windows 7 without Aero; you just won't have access to Aero's features, meaning you'll be missing out on much of the visual appeal to Windows 7.

In a case like this, you need to figure out how you're going to resolve the problem before moving forward. How exactly you resolve the problem with a system will vary. You might, for example, be able to use updated drivers from the manufacturer. You might find a documented workaround online. Or you may well wind up having to upgrade select portions of your computer hardware to a new version that has Windows 7 drivers. In the example shown in Figure 3.4, you might need to buy a new video card that has a Windows 7 driver if you can't find a suitable driver online. In the most extreme cases, you might need to buy a new computer, but as long as your system meets the specifications outlined in Chapter 1, that probably won't be necessary.

This system
passed all tests

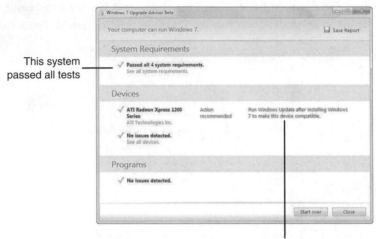

The Advisor recommends running
Windows update after Windows 7 is installed

FIGURE 3.3

This system passed the Windows Update Advisor's tests (although it recommends running Windows Update after Windows 7 is installed to update the video driver).

This system
failed a test

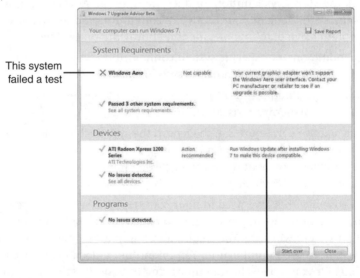

The Advisor recommends contacting
the PC manufacturer for an upgrade

FIGURE 3.4

This system failed the Windows Update Advisor test.

What we suggest doing, however, is saving the Windows Update Advisor reports for each system on which you want to install Windows 7 so that you can refer to them as part of your update process, resolving any problems that are reported. Having done that, you should go through your system and determine what applications are installed, so you can make sure they're reinstalled after you get into Windows 7.

Migrating Applications from Windows XP to Windows 7

The next task is to use the Windows Easy Transfer Wizard to move your application and user data from the old Windows XP installation into the Windows 7 installation. In this section, we'll discuss how to move your application data out of Windows XP so that it will be available for installation into Windows 7.

First, download and install the Windows Easy Transfer Wizard. Point your browser to www.microsoft.com, hover your mouse over the Downloads and Trials button, and from the drop-down menu that appears select Download Center. Then, in the search box, type `Windows Easy Transfer Wizard` and press Enter.

We suggest that you download the installer to your system before running it, rather than running it directly from the download link. Why? Because you're going to need to install it again when you move your application profiles into the Windows 7 installation.

Although the Easy Transfer Wizard asks for a data transfer cable, you don't need one; in fact, many of the more efficient methods don't use the data transfer cable. We recommend the following:

- If you're moving your applications from Windows XP on one computer to Windows 7 on a new computer, you should use the network transfer mode.
- If you're moving your applications from Windows XP to Windows 7 on the same computer, you should use the CD/DVD/removable media option.

The only time we've found the data transfer cable to be superior is when you are migrating between two computers, without any networking capability. If networking is available, we'll use it, for the simple reason that transfers over Fast Ethernet are much faster than using the transfer cable.

One thing we've found very useful for same-system transfers like this is a suitably sized flash drive, or a USB external hard disk. The reason for using an external drive of this sort is that it allows you to wipe and rewrite the computer's internal hard disk—which is actually a very good idea under most circumstances. A decent USB external disk can be had online for under $50, with enough room to move most system installations. This approach has three other benefits:

- You can easily archive the system state before reinstalling applications and the like by simply copying the archive files, to a file server, to DVDs, or to another storage drive.

- You can reuse the same external drive as you upgrade multiple computers—upgrade one, erase the data, move on to the next computer, and so on.

- After all your migrating is done, you can use the same external drive as a backup device.

note

From this point forward, our examples are based on the assumption that you are installing Windows 7 on the same computer on which you have Windows XP installed and that you have a suitable external drive.

About Partitions

Computer hard disks are defined both by their physical capabilities and by the logical breakdown of those capabilities. The logical breakdown is referred to as partitioning and involves creating logical "drives" that your computer recognizes as separate disk drives. The best analogy is to think of your house—the physical drive is the building, while each logical drive would be a separate room.

That being said, for almost all normal users, there is no real reason to create multiple partitions on your hard disk, other than those that your Windows 7 system installation requires (such as a separate recovery partition). The reason for this is that virtually anything that can be done with a partition, you can also do with folders, which are less of an issue to manage. Thus, using the default partitioning scheme that the Windows 7 installer creates is probably your best approach.

If, however, you know what you are doing with regard to disk partitioning, feel free to adjust the partition tables as appropriate to your system requirements. Some more advanced users do create separate partitions for their Windows operating system and data files (music, photos, documents, and so on). Doing so allows you to reinstall a good Windows installation gone bad without needing to back up and restore all of your data files.

For a short discussion of disk partitioning, and some of its benefits, see http://en.wikipedia.org/wiki/Disk_partitioning.

After you've installed Windows Easy Transfer Wizard, your next step is to start transferring files:

1. Close all the applications currently open on the computer, and start the Easy Transfer Wizard (see Figure 3.5).

FIGURE 3.5

Windows Easy Transfer Wizard.

2. Click Next. The file transfer methods screen appears.

3. Select an external hard disk or flash drive.

4. Easy Transfer asks if this is your old or new computer. Select This Is My Old Computer (see Figure 3.6).

FIGURE 3.6

Selecting the computer from which you are transferring files.

5. Select what you want to transfer (see Figure 3.7).

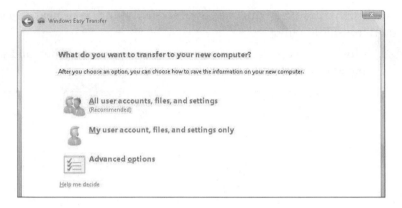

FIGURE 3.7

Choose the files that you want to transfer from your XP installation to your Windows 7 installation.

tip

We've been using the Easy Transfer Wizard for quite a while, and we've found that it's much easier to migrate all user accounts, files, and settings and then clean up any potential issues after the migration. If, however, you want fine-grained control over your migration, you can use the My User Account, Files, and Settings Only option to migrate a single user account, or the Advanced Options option for custom migrations.

Think Carefully About the Files You Back Up

If you're like most of us, you've been using your computer for quite a while, accumulating pictures, documents, video, music, spreadsheet files, a greeting card database, and assorted other files. Those files are important to you, and easily overlooked in an upgrade when you're paying attention to things such as system files and application programs. Don't forget your documents, photos, music files, and the like!

For instance:

- Check the location of your Internet Explorer email files. When you installed IE, you were asked to specify where to store files that will show up within IE as being in your Inbox, Sent, Trash, and other folders. If you've set up a location other than the defaults, make sure these files are included in the transfer.

- You have probably generated a huge number of documents, spreadsheets, presentations, and other data files and they're not all stored under My Documents, although you may have some files stored there, too. Unless you want to risk losing these files, make sure they're included in the transfer.

- Is all of your stored music in the My Music folder, or have you stored some of your tunes elsewhere? If you have created playlists in your music player, look at your music player's documentation to see if those playlists can be transferred or exported so that you can back them up, too.

- The My Pictures folder might include a lot of your photos and other pictures, but you've probably stored some of your pictures in other folders, particularly if you've used more than one application program to process your pictures. Be sure to check all the non-default folders where those important pictures might be stored and include them in the transfer.

- If you've been using a previous version of Media Center, your picture, music, and video files may have been stored separately. Make sure they are transferred.

- If you have partitioned your hard disk into two or more virtual hard disks (such as Drive F: and Drive G:, for instance), it can be easy to forget to look at the folders on those disks when you're compiling the list of files to transfer. Be sure to include them.

- You don't have to include files on removable media, such as thumb drives. If they're not plugged into the computer when you go through the upgrade process, they should still be readable when the upgrade is finished.

6. When you're ready, click Next.

    Before performing the transfer, the Easy Transfer Wizard gives you an opportunity to review what is being migrated (see Figure 3.8). Check through the list to make sure you haven't missed something important; then click Next to start the migration process.

    In the example in Figure 3.8, the user has assembled all of the files he wants to save in the folder "Joel" to make the transfer easy. This screen may not look the same way if you've chosen multiple folders and files from different locations.

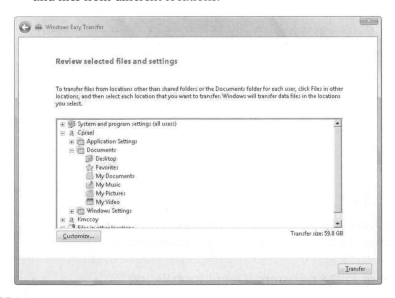

FIGURE 3.8

Review the files and settings you have elected to transfer and give your new overall transfer file a name.

7. When the Easy Transfer Wizard is finished, check your external drive to make sure that the settings files were stored properly. You should find a .MIG file with the name you gave it earlier (see Figure 3.9). Depending on what you have on your system, the migration file may easily be several hundred megabytes (or even gigabytes).

---

tip

One way to make your transfer a bit easier at this point is to copy the Windows Easy Transfer Wizard installer onto the external drive. That way, you can easily load it after you've installed Windows 7.

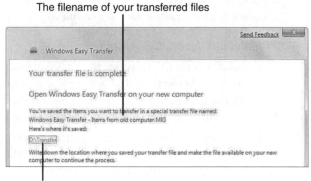

The filename of your transferred files

The location in which your transferred files are saved

FIGURE 3.9

Here you can see the files that were transferred and the location in which they were saved.

---

caution

You need to be aware of one issue: Windows Easy Transfer doesn't move applications; it moves only their settings. This makes for a much smaller migration package, but it has its own issues. We'll discuss some of the pros and cons of this approach in Chapter 8, along with some methods of directly migrating applications.

Installing Windows 7

You are now ready to install Windows 7. Boot from your Windows 7 installation DVD, and perform a new installation.

How to Do a Custom (Clean) Installation

Follow these steps to perform a clean installation:

caution

A clean installation consists of removing all data from your hard disk by reparti-
tioning and reformatting your hard disk and reinstalling the operating system
and programs to an empty (clean) hard disk. This means that any programs or
data you might have still stored on that hard disk will be removed and you
won't have access to them any more, unless you've previously copied those programs and data to a separate place, such as another virtual or real hard disk,
another place on your network, or to a temporary storage device such as a USB
thumb drive or other removable material. A clean installation also offers you an
opportunity to clean up space on your hard disk, storing the programs you
decide to reinstall in a more efficient manner and perhaps compacting some of
your data files. However, the most common mistake people make prior to a
clean installation is not saving everything they want to keep. Be sure you select
all the files you even *think* you may want to keep. You can delete the ones you
truly don't need later.

1. Insert the Windows 7 installation disc into the computer's DVD drive,
   turn on your computer, and then do one of the following:

   - If you want to replace your computer's existing operating sys-
     tem with Windows 7, and you don't need to adjust your disk
     partitions, go to step 2.

   - Restart your computer with the installation disc inserted in
     your DVD drive. If you're asked to press a key to boot from the
     DVD, press the appropriate key. If the Install Windows window
     appears as shown in Figure 3.10, go to step 2.

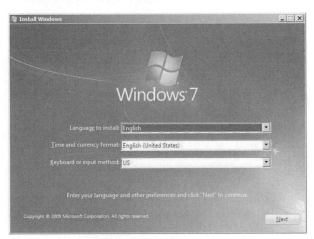

FIGURE 3.10

If you see the Install Windows window, you can go on to the next step.

note

If the Install Windows page doesn't appear and you're not asked to press a key to start from DVD, you might have to specify that your computer use its DVD drive as the startup device. You'll need to restart your computer, enter the BIOS Setup, specify your DVD drive as the startup device, and then start Windows from the Windows 7 installation DVD as described previously. See your computer's documentation for entering the BIOS setup (this varies from computer to computer). Or, watch closely while your computer is booting. Before the Windows 7 splash screen appears, several lines of text appear quickly on your screen. In the text, you should see directions, such as Press F2 to Enter BIOS Setup. Press whatever key is specified. Once the BIOS Setup appears, you will need to scan around and look for boot drive options and set yours to look in your DVD drive first for a bootable DVD. Be careful with the BIOS settings and if you make changes that you are certain aren't correct, exit the BIOS without saving. If you are sure that you have changed the boot order correctly, be sure to choose the exit and save option. It's nearly impossible to give specific directions for this procedure because it varies from BIOS to BIOS. If you are uncertain what to do, we suggest contacting your computer's manufacturer.

2. When the Install Windows page appears, click Install Now.

3. When the Get Important Updates for Installation page appears, click Get the Latest Updates as shown in Figure 3.11. Among other things, the latest updates will help protect your computer from recently detected security problems.

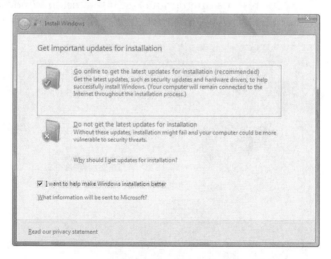

FIGURE 3.11

Be sure to download and install all important updates right away.

4. After the updates are complete, resume the Windows 7 installation by clicking the Continue button. Click I Accept the License Terms (you must accept to continue the installation) and click Next.

5. When the Which Type of Installation Do You Want? page appears, click Custom.

6. When the Where Do You Want to Install Windows? page appears, choose one of the following options:

   - If you don't want to specify a specific partition where you want to install Windows, or create partitions on your hard disk, click Next.

   - If you already have an existing partition where you want to install Windows 7 to create a multiple boot configuration, select that partition and click Next to begin the installation. (Be sure to install Windows 7 on a *different* partition from where your current version of Windows XP is installed.)

   - If you want to create, extend, delete, or format a partition, click Drive Options (Advanced), select the option you want, and follow the instructions. Click Next to begin the installation. (If the Drive Options (Advanced) option is disabled, you will have to start your computer using the installation disc.)

   - If you have only a single partition defined for the disk, you will need to delete it and then create a blank disk partition.

---

note

You might see a window that says the partition you selected contains files from a previous Windows installation. If you want to proceed, these files will be moved to a folder called Windows.old and will be accessible but not used to run Windows 7.

---

7. Click OK.

8. Your computer will begin installing the Windows 7 files and may stop and start several times (see Figure 3.12). You can see that the system is busy when an ellipse (...) appears after the phrase describing its current action.

---

note

The installation can take a long time (25 minutes is not unreasonable for certain configurations); it depends on the speed of your CPU, the speed of your DVD reader, and several other factors.

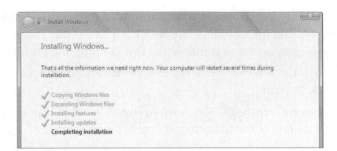

FIGURE 3.12
The installation process might take a while, so get comfortable.

9. When installation has completed, you'll see the new Windows 7 desktop. The first thing you will note is that the desktop interface has changed quite a bit from Windows XP. It is, however, quite similar to that introduced in Windows Vista. To learn more about new features that are part of Windows 7, see Chapters 6 to11.

Migrating Your Applications from XP to Windows 7

After you've installed Windows 7 on the computer, you are ready to start putting applications back on and configuring it for use. Broadly speaking, you'll do two things:

-   Install applications from your checklist.
-   Reload application and user profiles using Windows Easy Transfer.

Installing Applications

Earlier in this chapter, after you ran Windows Update Advisor, you might recall that we had you create a list of all the applications on the computer. This list also appeared in Chapter 1 when you were planning your migration. Now is the time to use that list. Use it as a checklist to make sure that you install all the applications you want on your computer. The good thing is that for every application that you are reinstalling, you do not need to worry about reconfiguration. Further, you don't have to worry about creating unique user profiles.

In each case, load the application, run it to resolve any registration issues, and keep going. Do not spend time customizing the application to deal with specific user preferences at this point. Your goal should be to have loaded, running, properly licensed software.

Reloading Application and User Profiles

After you have loaded your applications, you need to reload the application and user profiles:

1. The first thing to do is hook up your external drive to the computer again. Make sure that it connects properly to Windows 7 and that its contents are visible to the computer.

2. Go onto the disk and install Windows Easy Transfer Wizard under Windows 7. You've already done this once, and this is why we had you save the downloaded installer and put it on that external drive.

3. As shown in Figure 3.13, start the Easy Transfer Wizard, the same as under Windows XP (described earlier in this chapter).

FIGURE 3.13

Starting Windows Easy Transfer Wizard for moving your files into Windows 7.

4. From the select computer window you saw in Figure 3.6, select This Is My New Computer.

5. Windows Easy Transfer will ask you if the files are already saved to an external drive. Select Yes and point Easy Transfer to where you have stored the migration (.MIG) file.

tip

Before it migrates the files, Windows Easy Transfer allows you to review the settings and files you want to migrate. If you are new to this, leave everything selected. If you feel you need finer-grain control, however, use the Advanced Options to selectively install the migrated settings onto the Windows 7 installation.

6. After your transfer is complete, Windows Easy Transfer displays a Transfer Completed window, allowing you to review what's been installed.

7. One very useful feature of this is that it also creates a transfer report showing all the applications for which settings were transferred. You can use this report to verify that the applications you installed covered all the bases as far as what was supposed to be installed.

Resolving Application Upgrades and Cross-Grades

As we noted in Chapter 1, a significant upgrade like this is a good time to also deal with application upgrades and cross-grades. As you may recall, we suggested you plan out your upgrades and cross-grades so you could be sure of what you were doing and what needed to be done at each step in the process.

You also need to pay attention to timing at this point. We suggest that you hold off resolving application upgrades and cross-grades until after you have migrated your application and user data from your Windows XP installation. The reason is that upgrades and cross-grades will frequently convert user parameters to be appropriate to the new version of the application software. If you install the upgrade or cross-grade first and then perform your migration, you may accidentally wind up with corrupted application settings.

If, on the other hand, you perform the migration first and then deal with the upgrade or cross-grade, you can be sure that upgrade tools correctly pick up and handle your application and user profile data, resulting in a clean installation.

4

Migrating from Vista to Windows 7

We're going to assume you have read at least Chapters 1 and 2 (and it's not a bad idea to skim Chapter 8) before turning to this chapter. We're also assuming that you've assessed what application programs you have and the appropriate versions of them you want to use with Windows 7. If you followed the instructions in Chapters 1 and 2, you've verified that you have the hardware you need, you have the existing version of Vista (including the latest service pack upgrades), and you've evaluated the options for upgrading your applications (with the form shown at Table 2.1).

Because most users will be using Windows 7 on a PC, the instructions given in this chapter focus on procedures in that environment. Although probably similar, the procedures for installing Windows 7 on a Mac or under Linux are beyond the scope of this book.

Documenting Your Vista System

In Chapter 1, we suggested that you note your version and service pack level for Vista (see Tables 1.1 through 1.4). In that exercise, you noted other information about your system, including the amount of available disk space, the amount of memory, and other useful information. The installation process is where you'll be using that information.

What You Need to Have on Hand

In Chapter 1 you made some notes about what your system included. Your system properties screen looked something like that shown in Figure 1.2. Have those notes on hand. You also made some notes about your applications programs, on a screen like that shown in Figure 1.3. Have those notes on hand, too.

Performing the Migration to Windows 7

When upgrading from Windows Vista to Windows 7, you have two types of installation to choose from:

- **Clean installation**—A clean install deletes everything on your hard drive and places a copy of Windows 7 on the drive. That means anything on the hard drive that isn't backed up elsewhere is lost forever. Clean installs are the most hassle, but many experts prefer it because it gives them a chance to start with a fresh, clean installation of Windows; a freshly formatted drive; and a chance to start over with a PC that isn't bogged down with extra unused software and the like.

caution

If you are considering a clean install, it is imperative that you back up any data files that you want to have after Windows 7 is installed. Anything that isn't backed up will be gone forever. Don't say we didn't warn you.

- **Upgrade installation**—An upgrade installation does just that: it upgrades your current Windows Vista installation while preserving your data files.

Installing Windows 7

Follow these steps to install Windows 7:

1. Insert the Windows 7 installation disc into the computer's DVD drive, turn on your computer, and then do one of the following:

   - If you want to replace your computer's existing operating system with Windows 7 and you don't need to adjust your disk partitions, go to step 2.

   - If your computer doesn't have an operating system installed, or you want to install Windows 7 on another disk partition, restart your computer with the installation disc inserted in your CD or DVD drive. If you're asked to press a key to boot from DVD or CD, press any key. If the Install Windows page appears as shown in Figure 4.1, go to step 2.

Forcing Windows to Boot from the Windows 7 DVD

If the Install Windows page doesn't appear and you're not asked to press a key to start from DVD, you might have to specify that your computer use its DVD drive as the startup device. You'll need to restart your computer, press the indicated key to enter your system BIOS (usually either F2 or DEL), find the appropriate section in the BIOS to specify your system's boot order, and then specify your DVD drive as the startup device. Unless you know what you are doing, do not change any other settings while doing this—this is a surefire way to render your system unusable. Once you have changed the boot order setting to allow you to boot from your DVD drive, save the settings and exit BIOS. This will restart your system again, and you should then be able to start Windows from the Windows 7 installation DVD as described previously. See your computer's documentation for entering the BIOS setup (this varies from computer to computer). Or, watch closely while your computer is booting. Before the Windows 7 splash screen appears, several lines of text appear quickly on your screen. In the text, you should see directions, such as "Press F2 to Enter BIOS Setup." Press whatever key is specified. Once the BIOS Setup appears, you will need to scan around and look for boot drive options and set yours to look in your DVD drive first for a bootable DVD. Be careful with the BIOS settings and if you make changes that you are certain aren't correct, exit the BIOS without saving. If you are sure that you have changed the boot order correctly, be sure to choose the exit and save option. It's nearly impossible to give specific directions for this procedure because it varies from BIOS to BIOS. If you are uncertain what to do, we suggest contacting your computer's manufacturer.

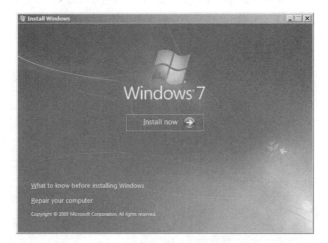

FIGURE 4.1

This screen appears after you've booted your PC with the Windows 7 installation disc.

About Partitions

Computer hard disks are defined both by their physical capabilities and by the logical breakdown of those capabilities. The logical breakdown is referred to as partitioning and involves creating logical "drives" that your computer recognizes as separate disk drives. The best analogy is to think of your house—the physical drive is the building, while each logical drive would be a separate room.

That being said, for almost all normal users, there is no real reason to create multiple partitions on your hard disk, other than those that your Windows 7 system installation requires (such as a separate recovery partition). The reason for this is that virtually anything that can be done with a partition, you can also do with folders, which are less of an issue to manage. Thus, using the default partitioning scheme that the Windows 7 installer creates is probably your best approach.

If, however, you know what you are doing with regard to disk partitioning, feel free to adjust the partition tables as appropriate to your system requirements. Some more advanced users do create separate partitions for their Windows operating system and data files (music, photos, documents, and so on). Doing so allows you to reinstall a good Windows installation gone bad without needing to back up and restore all of your data files.

For a short discussion of disk partitioning, and some of its benefits, see http://en.wikipedia.org/wiki/Disk_partitioning.

2. When the Install Windows page appears, click Install Now.

3. When the Get Important Updates for Installation page appears, click Get the Latest Updates (as shown in Figure 4.2). Among other things, the latest updates help protect your computer from recently detected security problems.

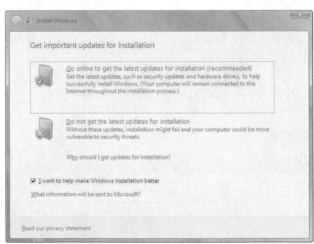

FIGURE 4.2

Be sure to download any available updates from Microsoft during the installation process.

4. After the updates are complete, resume the Windows 7 installation by clicking the Continue button. Click I Accept the License Terms (you must accept to continue the installation) and click Next.

How to Perform a Custom (Clean) Installation

Use the following steps to perform a clean installation:

1. When the Which Type of Installation Do You Want? page appears, click Custom.

2. When the Where Do You Want to Install Windows? page appears, choose one of the following options:

    *   If you don't want to specify a specific partition where you want to install Windows or to create partitions on your hard disk, click Next.

    *   If you already have an existing partition where you want to install Windows 7 to create a multiple boot configuration (meaning that you want to be able to run Windows Vista or Windows 7), select that partition and click Next to begin the installation. (Be sure to install Windows 7 on a different partition from where your current version of Windows Vista is installed.)

    *   If you want to create, extend, delete, or format a partition, click Drive Options (Advanced), select the option you want, and follow the instructions. Click Next to begin the installation.

note

If the Drive Options (Advanced) option is disabled, it means that you started the installation of Windows 7 while your current version of Windows Vista was running; to alter partitions, you need to stop the installation, power down your computer, insert the Windows 7 disc into the drive, and restart using the Windows 7 disc.

tip

You might see a window that indicates the partition you selected contains files from a previous Windows installation. If you want to proceed, these files will be moved to a folder called Windows.old and will be accessible but not used to run Windows 7.

3. After you are done setting up partitions, click OK.

From this point on, the instructions for completing a Windows 7 installation are the same for both a clean install and an upgrade. Please see
"Finishing the Installation" later in this chapter.

How to Perform an Upgrade Installation

Use the following steps to upgrade your existing Windows Vista installation to Windows 7.

> ### caution
>
> IMPORTANT: Before you begin the upgrade process, you must have downloaded
> and installed either Vista Service Pack 1 and Service Pack 2. The upgrade soft-
> ware will not work unless the Service Pack has been installed.

1. With your current version of Windows Vista running, insert the
    Windows 7 installation disk into your computer's DVD drive.

2. The Install Windows page appears; click Install Now.

3. The screen displays questions about running Setup; click the Setup
    option.

4. The Get Important Updates for Installation page appears; click Get
    the Latest Updates. This may take a while. Note that if you have not
    included the Service Pack 1 or 2 upgrades, you'll be directed to down-
    load and install the upgrades. If you don't do it now, the installer
    program will bug you again shortly, so you might as well do it now.
    It's important!

5. The Please Read the License Terms page appears. Click I Accept the
    License Terms (you must accept to continue the installation) and
    click Next.

6. The Which Type of Installation Do You Want? page appears; click
    Upgrade.

7. If you haven't upgraded your version of Vista to include Service Pack
    1, you'll see a compatibility report and a request to use Windows 7
    Upgrade Advisor. Click the Download button.

8. Double-click the Windows 7 Upgrade Advisor button to open the pro-
    gram (see Figure 4.3).

9. When asked to check if your PC is ready for Windows 7, click the
    Start Check button. The Upgrade Advisor will check for compatibility
    issues. The Upgrade Advisor will report any unmet system require-
    ments or incompatibility issues. This report will list both mandated
    and optional upgrades, such as upgrading your copy of Windows 7

to Windows 7 Professional, Ultimate, or Enterprise (see Figure 4.4).
Click the appropriate links to deal with these issues.

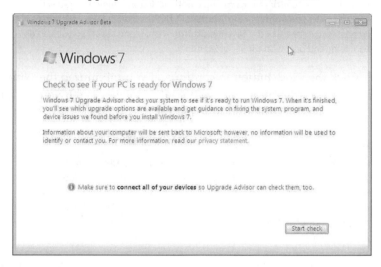

FIGURE 4.3

*Use the Windows Upgrade Advisor to check for any compatibility issues with your new
Windows 7 installation.*

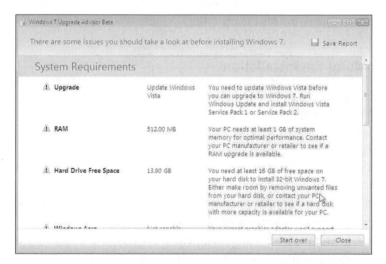

FIGURE 4.4

The Windows Upgrade Advisor will help you sort out any incompatibilities.

tip

If the Upgrade Advisor reports multiple optional issues—meaning issues that won't prevent you from running Windows 7, but could affect your overall usability or enjoyment—click the Save Report icon to store the report so you can go back later and deal with the reported items.

10. Click the Close button to continue. If you minimized the Windows 7 Upgrade Advisor, maximize it again. When asked if you want to continue, click the Continue button.

note

If you have paused (for instance, overnight) in your upgrade of Vista to include Service Pack 1 or 2, you might be asked to check again for recent upgrades. Follow the instructions to download and install the upgrades. Your computer might need to shut down and restart during this process. DO NOT turn off your computer during this process. The activity LEDs on your computer will tell you that your machine is still running, even if the screen is black.

11. When asked if you want to Run or Save the Windows 7 Upgrade Advisor, click Run unless you want to save the Advisor and run it later. (You might want to do an installation now and get back later to the non-critical items identified by the Upgrade Advisor, in which case you will want to click the Save the Windows 7 Upgrade option.)

Finishing the Installation

If you've gotten past the Upgrade Advisor, you're now ready to finish installing Windows 7.

If you've clicked the Run button, your computer will begin installing the Windows 7 files and might stop and restart several times (see Figure 4.5). You can see that the system is busy when an ellipse (...) appears after the phrase describing its current action. This step can take a long time (25 minutes is not unreasonable for certain configurations) and depends on the speed of your CPU, the speed of your DVD reader, and several other factors.

When installation has completed, you'll see the new Windows 7 desktop. Your desktop will appear with the defaults you selected:

1. When the Installation Complete window appears, click the Close button.

2. Eventually your computer will begin installing the Windows 7 files and may stop and start several times. You can see that the system is busy when an ellipse (...) appears after the phrase describing its current action.

FIGURE 4.5

Windows will keep you posted on its progress during the installation process.

> **note**
>
> The installation of Windows 7 can take a long time (25 minutes is not unreason-
> able for certain configurations) and depends on the speed of your CPU, the
> speed of your DVD reader, and several other factors.

3. When prompted, enter your Windows Product Key. This will either be
   in the product box or on the case in which the DVD came. You will
   need to enter a combination of letters and numbers like this:

   XXXX-XXXX-XXXX-XXXX-XXXX

4. When asked, choose the security setting option you want. To get
   started immediately, select Ask Me Later. If you want to set your
   security options now, click one of the buttons shown in Figure 4.6:

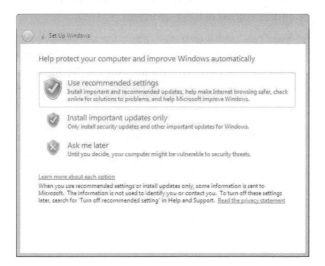

FIGURE 4.6

Setting up security is an important step of the installation process.

- **Use Recommended Settings**—Choose this option if you want to use the default security settings. These settings are ones that most users will want. You can change your security settings later after installation. See Chapter 8, "Security," for more information.

- **Install Important Updates Only**—Choose this option if you want to install only the most important updates from the list that the Upgrade Advisor identified. These can affect system performance and might include critical updates to your system software. Other updates will be identified as not as critical, meaning that you can install them later, if you choose.

- **Ask Me Later**—Choose this option if you feel it's important to proceed with installation immediately.

caution

Choose this option only if you've already looked at the list of updates from Upgrade Advisor and have determined that none of them are critical. If there are critical updates and you don't install them, you might leave your system open to attack from the outside during the installation process.

5. When asked about what kind of network you are using, choose either Home or Work. The difference is largely related to what servers and other devices are expected to be available as you use Windows 7.

    - **Home**—A home network generally consists of one or two computers connected to a printer.

    - **Work**—A work network generally means that there are one or more servers to which one or more computers are connected. These servers are usually responsible for files not stored on the individual computers, for handling printing, or for handling email.

6. Finally, you'll see a message indicating Windows 7 is ready for you to use, and to tailor as you see fit. Your screen will look something like that shown in Figure 4.7.

FIGURE 4.7

The finished Windows 7 installation (though your desktop background might be different).

5

Application and Data Migration

One issue that comes up regularly when dealing with operating system upgrades is moving your data from your old system installation to your new system installation.

Which Approach to Use?

There are two basic approaches to application and data migration.

- The first is to reinstall your applications and then migrate your application settings and data. We discussed this in some detail in Chapter 2, "Applications."

- The second, which we have found to be much more straightforward and easy to execute, is to use an application migration package to move your applications, their settings, and your data into your new system installation.

Previously, in Chapter 2, we demonstrated how you would perform the first of these two approaches—reinstalling applications and migrating application settings and data. In this chapter, we'll focus on the second of these two approaches—using a migration package to do the heavy lifting for you.

Choosing the Right Migration Package

Choosing the right migration tool depends on which approach you choose. If you have decided to migrate only your application settings and data, you would do well to use the suite of free Microsoft migration tools, including specifically the Windows Transfer Wizard. We discussed this in some detail in Chapter 2.

If, however, you have decided to go ahead and migrate everything, you will want a dedicated application migration tool. We have found several good ones:

- **Windows EasyTransfer**—This transfer package is a free download-able package from Microsoft that is useful for bulk file transfers and application settings. It is not capable of transferring applications, which we see as a significant limitation. We discussed it in some detail in Chapters 3 and 4.

- **Laplink PCmover**—This is an application migration package avail-able from LapLink Software.(www.laplink.com/pcmover/). PC Mover includes a special add-on capability to perform in-place upgrades from Windows XP to Windows 7. Although Microsoft does not sup-port this, Laplink has added this capability to the newest version of their software. Because of this, we are including a special section describing the PC Mover's in-place upgrade functionality at the end of this chapter.

- **AlohaBob PC Relocator**—This software package was formerly pro-duced by Apptimum Software. In early 2006, Microsoft bought Apptimum, and PC Relocator stopped being sold. However, copies of PC Relocator are still available through various online sources, including Amazon. A quick Google search for "PC Relocator price" turned up multiple vendors with new and used copies. Ironically, the technology in PC Relocator is what is behind the Windows Transfer Wizard. The differences are that Microsoft has updated the Transfer Wizard to better handle Vista-based applications, and it has removed the application migration technology from PC Relocator, leaving the application settings and data migration capabilities.

Depending on the type of migration you are performing, you may also need some extra hardware. At various times, we've used the following:

- A network link between the two computers involved
- A USB link cable
- A USB thumb drive and/or external hard disk
- A DVD-ROM drive and media

In the following sections, we'll discuss various approaches and demon-strate how each of these packages works.

General Considerations

Broadly speaking, you will do the same thing for each application migration situation: You use the app migration software to move a group of files that contain all the user accounts, application files, settings, and data files that are stored on your computer to the new system, installing all the applications exactly the way they were installed on the original system.

This gets a bit more complicated in the process of moving the information from your old system to the new system. When you are dealing with two physical computers, the primary issue becomes one of transporting the information from one computer to another. When you have a single physical computer, the challenge becomes one of protecting the information while you install the new operating system.

One complication in all this comes with regard to licensing rules. As a rule, OEM (original equipment manufacturer—the company that built your computer) licenses are bound to a single, physical computer. Retail licenses (software bought from a store or online) are not. So you should pay attention to your licensing restrictions when migrating applications. But, just to illustrate:

- If you wanted to upgrade a Windows XP system to Windows 7, you would be forced to install a new copy of Windows 7, rather than upgrading XP to 7. In that case, you would want to use application migration software to move your applications, even though you were using the same physical computer. But because you were keeping the same computer, your OEM license would still be valid.

- If you wanted to upgrade to a new computer, along with migrating to Windows 7, you would probably not be able to take your OEM software with you—though this rule generally isn't applicable to older software, and useful enforcement mechanisms, such as online license key checking, are relatively new.

- Continuing to use the same software on an older computer, after you have migrated it to a new computer, would almost certainly be a license violation—though some software is licensed on a "per user" not "per system" basis. If you continue to use the software on the old computer, you might wind up with compliance problems, particularly if you use the vendor's online customer service facilities.

tip

One thing you should definitely do before starting a migration is to familiarize yourself with how the migration software works. If a manual came with the software, read it. If not, when you first install the software, look for a tutorial or help system and read that. Migration is one of those cases where "forewarned is fore-armed."

Migrating Data on a Single Computer

The first example we'll look at is migrating data from one system installation to another on the same computer. Before you begin, you need to gather a little information about your computer and use that to make sure that you have the right resources available. The basic problem you need to resolve is determining where are you going to store your applications and data. You can choose from two options:

- If you have a CD-RW or DVD-RW drive (in other words, a drive capable of both reading *and writing* either CDs or DVDs), you can burn the information to one or more CDs/DVDs. This has the added advantage of giving you a permanent application backup. Remember, however, that each DVD-ROM only has a capacity of 4.7GB and CDs have far less.

- If you have an external hard disk or a thumb drive with sufficient capacity, you can store the application data there.

tip

Although the procedures in this section mostly apply to Windows XP migrations, they are equally applicable to Windows Vista systems. The caveat there, however, is that they only apply to Vista systems in the event that you are performing a new installation. If you are upgrading from Windows Vista to Windows 7, all of the application and data migration is handled as part of the upgrade process, and you do not need to migrate your applications or data.

If you decide to store your application data on an external drive, you should first check to ensure that you have sufficient capacity:

1. Click Start and choose My Computer.

2. Select Local Disk (C:) or whatever drive contains the data you want to migrate.

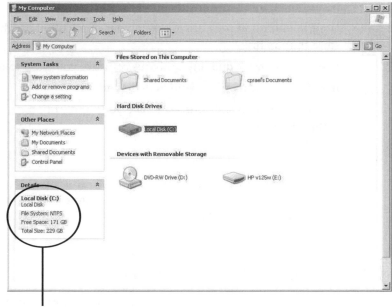

The total capacity of the drive as well
as the available space is shown here.

FIGURE 5.1

Selecting the drive shows the drive capacity information you need before migrating data.

3. In the lower-left corner, in the Details pane, you will see some basic information about your hard disk, including its total size and the amount of free space it has left (see Figure 5.1). Subtract the free space from the total size to see how much disk space you are currently using. In this case, subtracting 171GB from 229GB means that we are currently using 58GB of space on this system's disk.

4. Compare the amount of disk space you are using with the capacity of the external hard disk or thumb drive that you plan to use to store your system image. In this example, a 60GB external disk would be sufficient to move everything, whereas a 16GB thumb drive would not. Alternatively, if we were to use DVD-ROMs, we would need a total of 13 DVD-ROMs to store the entire application plus data backup. We arrived at this determination by dividing 58GB (the amount of data we want to move) by 4.7GB per DVD, which comes out to 12.34, or 13 DVDs.

When you have all the equipment and supplies you will need, you can get started. Broadly speaking, you perform five tasks to migrate your applications:

- Install the migration software on your existing system.
- Use the migration software to create your application archive, and store that archive.
- Install Windows 7 and any antivirus software you want to run.
- Install the migration software under Windows 7.
- Use the migration software to retrieve your application archive and install it under Windows 7.

---

note

One limitation you should be aware of is that, at least as far as PC Relocator is concerned, it is not capable of migrating security software. Therefore, this is the one type of software that you must manually install, preferably before you install your other migrated software.

Task 1: Install the Migration Software

Installing the migration software is easy. For this example, we installed PC Relocator using the following steps:

1. Place the PC Relocator CD in the system's CD- or DVD-ROM drive.

2. Run the Auto Installer.

3. Answer the installer's prompts as they come up.

Task 2: Create and Store Your Application Archive

Now we need to get started with the actual migration. One point you should note before beginning is that the relocation archive you create does not delete anything from your existing system configuration. It only copies and archives information.

1. Quit any other programs that you are running before starting PC Relocator.

2. Start PC Relocator Ultra Control. If, during the installation, you chose to have an icon for PC Relocator placed on your desktop, you can click it. If not, you'll need to navigate to the location in which you installed PC Relocator and run the application from there. After the program is launched, you will see the screen shown in Figure 5.2.

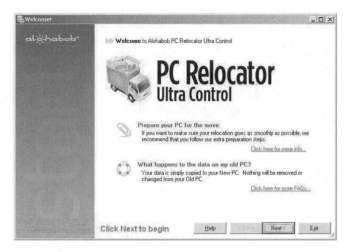

FIGURE 5.2

Although PC Relocator isn't being updated any longer, it's still a useful tool.

3. In previous years, you would use the Retrieve the Most Current Version capability to update your software before performing a migration. That option is no longer available, however, because the software is no longer being updated. If you allow the software to try to check for a new version, PC Relocator will lock up. Therefore, you should bypass the update by clicking the Next button.

4. You will receive a message indicating that to perform your backup, your system needs to shut off any other programs that are currently running. Allow PC Relocator to shut off these other programs, if you have not already done so.

5. You are asked if this is your old computer or your new one. Select Old PC, as shown in Figure 5.3, and then click Next.

6. Now you need to select your transfer method. Because you are transferring your applications to a new system installation on the same system, you need to select the CD/DVD or Other High Capacity Storage option as shown in Figure 5.4, and then click Next.

7. Now define the storage location for your application archive. If you are going to use an external disk drive of some sort, browse to the appropriate storage location on that external drive (as shown in Figure 5.5). A default name will be created for you, although you can change that name. If, on the other hand, you are using a CD/DVD drive, you should first insert a blank disk in the drive and then browse to that location.

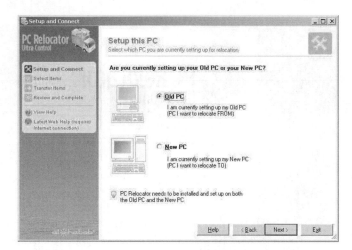

FIGURE 5.3

Choosing Old PC tells PC Relocator that you want to migrate data from this system installation to another.

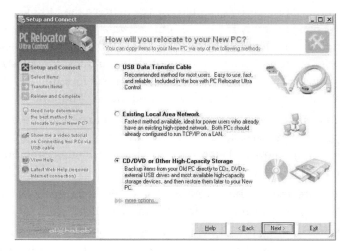

FIGURE 5.4

Because you are migrating applications from one system installation or another, you need to choose CD/DVD or Other High Capacity Storage.

8. In either case, after you have selected your location, click Next. As shown in Figure 5.6, PC Relocator performs a quick set of tests to make sure that the storage location is accessible and can be written to by the system.

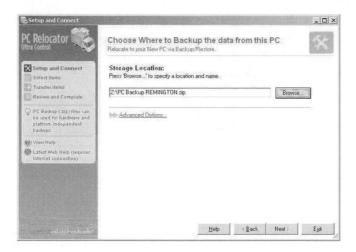

FIGURE 5.5

Choose where you want to store your application archive.

FIGURE 5.6

PC Relocator performs a few tests to make sure that the location in which you want to store your application archive is viable.

9. You are now ready for PC Relocator to scan your system to build a complete migration manifest. This manifest determines everything that is migrated—applications, settings, user information, and data files. Click Next to start the scan. Figure 5.7 shows a scan in progress. Depending on how much information is on your system, the scan may take quite a while (as in "overnight," so be sure to plan your time carefully).

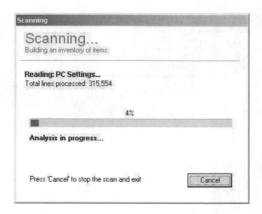

FIGURE 5.7

PC Relocator builds a manifest for all of the apps, settings, data files, and user information that will be migrated.

10. You need to choose the degree of control you want over your reloca-
    tion (see Figure 5.8). Depending on your experience and knowledge,
    you can select from the following:

    • **Automatic**—Allows PC Relocator to automatically select what
      programs to relocate and where to relocate them. If you are
      inexperienced in Windows system administration, we highly
      recommend that you select automatic and allow the software
      to handle this step.

    • **Standard Selectivity**—Provides a moderate degree of control
      over your migration. Use this setting if you are experienced in
      Windows system administration.

    • **Expert Selectivity**—Allows you complete control over your
      relocation, including retargeting of applications and on-the-fly
      relocation and reordering of files. Use this setting only if you
      are experienced in Windows system administration and you
      require the additional functionality. Click Next to continue.

11. Select the items that you want migrated. You will normally want to
    select Programs, Settings, and Files (see Figure 5.9). In addition, we
    have found it useful to leave SmartShield activated to provide a fil-
    tering medium against harmful viruses that might be hidden on
    your computer. Click Next.

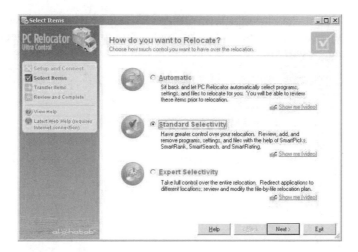

FIGURE 5.8

PC Relocator offers three levels of sensitivity when determining exactly what will be migrated.

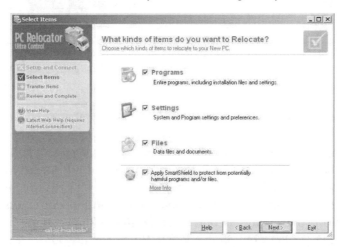

FIGURE 5.9

Choose the types of items you want migrated.

12. A software licensing compliance window pops up. Select Yes, I Agree that you will continue to abide by the licensing of any software that you have installed, that you want migrated, and then click the Continue button.

13. At this point, a listing of all items to be relocated appears (see Figure 5.10). This listing is based on the system scan performed in step 9. It

details every program, program setting, user setting, and file to be migrated. You can add items, remove items, and more from this review window.

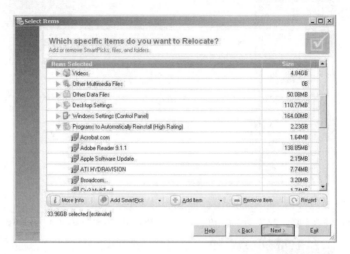

FIGURE 5.10

Check this list carefully to ensure that everything you want migrated is included here. If programs that you want reinstalled have a low rating, select Add SmartPick to mark them for reinstallation.

14.   When you are done reviewing, and possibly altering, your migration plan, click the Next button. When you do, a second review window appears, without the editing capability (see Figure 5.11). The ratings that you see reflect PC Relocator's estimate of the likelihood of successfully migrating a given piece of software. By default, only medium- and high-rated programs are reinstalled. Use this to confirm your migration, and if you see files or applications missing, click the Back button to revise it. When you are done, click Next.

15.   At this point, PC Relocator computes a pre-relocation summary, showing what it plans to relocate and how long it will take to do so (see Figure 5.12). This is the last stop before your actual relocation, so proceed by clicking Next only when you are ready to go ahead.

tip

We have found over time that the computed transfer estimate time tends to overstate how long a relocation will take. In this example, the computed time is 21 hours, 28 minutes. In reality, this will be done in about 6 hours.

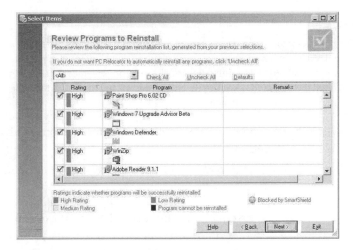

FIGURE 5.11

You get one last chance to check over what will be migrated.

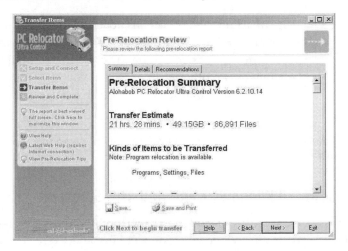

FIGURE 5.12

You'll see what is being transferred and how long it will take. As you can see, our migration would take more than 21 hours, so plan accordingly.

16. When you click Next on the Pre-relocation Review screen, PC Relocator begins creating your application archive. Generally speaking, you can leave the computer alone for this process (for systems with a large migration, we like to run this process overnight, when nobody is using the computer).

note

The one caveat to leaving the migration unattended is if you selected to use a CD or DVD burner for your storage, you will be regularly prompted to insert a new blank disk when the existing one is full. As you do, remember to label, tag, and mark the disks, and keep them in order—this will become important when you reinstall the application archive.

17. When PC Relocator is done creating your application archive, follow the prompts and exit the program.

18. Before doing anything else, verify that the application archive was, in fact, correctly created.

- If you are using an external disk, check that external disk and make sure that an archive file, with the name you gave it in step 7, actually exists. The file will likely be smaller than the value you calculated earlier than this chapter. But it should be there.

- If you are using CD/DVD ROMs, load the first disk and then browse to it and make sure that an archive file with the correct name from step 6 exists on the CD or DVD. You might want to check one or two other disks as well, if you have multiple disks, to make sure that the subsequent archives were correctly created.

After you have created and verified the application archive, you are ready to install Windows 7.

Task 3: Install Windows 7 and Antivirus Software

This task is the most irreversible step in the entire process. The reason is that when you install Windows 7, you will have effectively destroyed your old system installation. This is why you need to take such pains in creating and verifying the application archive before proceeding to this task.

caution

If you have not created and verified your application archive yet, as directed at the end of Task 2 earlier in this chapter, do so now.

Installing Windows 7 has already been discussed in Chapter 3, "Migrating from XP to Windows 7," and in Chapter 4, "Migrating from Vista to Windows 7." Follow the procedure in the appropriate chapter to install Windows 7 on your system. If you used an external drive to hold your application archive, you should detach it while you install Windows 7.

Reattach the drive at the end of this task, after you have installed Windows 7 and your security software (such as Norton or other antivirus, antispyware, and firewall software). At a minimum, you should make sure that Microsoft's built-in firewall is activated. To learn more about setting up security options, see Chapter 8, "Windows 7 Security."

After you have so installed Windows 7 and your security software, you need to deal with three more items:

- Configure your computer so your Internet connection is working properly.
- If you did not install Windows updates during the installation of Windows 7, go to http://update.microsoft.com/ and make sure that your computer has all necessary updates and patches.
- Install your chosen security software. If you are using third-party software, install that now, then activate it, and follow the instructions to make sure that you have the latest antivirus definitions. If you are using Microsoft's security software, make sure that it is fully activated and that it has the latest definitions. See Chapter 8 for more details on security.

At the end of this process, you will probably be asked to restart your computer, perhaps several times.

Task 4: Install the Migration Software Under Windows 7

As in Task 1, this task involves running the installer for your migration software. Now you are going to reinstall it under your new Windows 7 installation so that you can use it to install your application archive. In our case, follow these steps:

1. Place the PC Relocator CD in the system's CD- or DVD-ROM drive.

2. Run the Auto Installer.

3. Answer the installer's prompts as they come up.

Task 5: Use Migration Software to Install Your Application/Data Archive

Now we can get started with the other end of the migration process. If you are using an external drive, verify that it is hooked up to your computer and that the computer can recognize the data on the hard drive. If you are using CD or DVD discs, check several of the discs to make sure that your new system can read them. When you are ready to start, follow these steps:

1. Quit any other programs that you are running before starting PC
    Relocator.

2. Look for the PC Relocator Ultra Control icon on your desktop or
    wherever the program is installed on your hard drive, and double-
    click it.

3. Bypass the Retrieve the Most Current Version option, as you did early
    in this chapter in Task 2, by clicking the Next button.

4. You are prompted to close any open applications before performing
    the migration. Allow PC Relocator to shut off these other programs,
    if you have not already done so.

5. You are asked if this is your old computer or your new one (as shown
    in Figure 5.13). Select New PC, and then click Next.

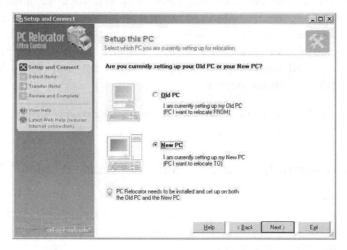

FIGURE 5.13

*Because you are installing the application on your newly minted Windows 7 computer, choose
New PC.*

6. Now you need to select your transfer method. Select the CD/DVD or
    Other High Capacity Storage option, and then click Next.

7. If you are using an external hard disk, browse to the location of your
    application archive file and select it. If you are using CD/DVD discs,
    place the first disc in the drive and then browse on that disc to the
    application archive file. In either case, after you have selected the
    application archive file, click Next.

8. At this point, the migration software takes over, migrating and
    installing your applications automatically. Just sit back and relax.

9. Once your application migration is complete, a report is generated showing what applications were migrated successfully and where you might have issues. You should review that report to verify that all of the applications and data that matter to you have been properly migrated.

note

If an important application doesn't migrate properly, your best bet is to try a direct re-installation of the application. Generally speaking, if the application migration software can't get it to work right, then you'll need the original installer to resolve the problem.

note

Also, depending on the software package, you might be required to re-enter the license key for your software. This is done to validate your software licensing and to bind the license key to the computer you are now using.

Migrating Applications and Data to a New Windows 7 Computer

The next example is migrating your information from an older computer, which could be an old Windows 2000 system, a Windows XP system, or a newer Windows Vista system, to a new, separate Windows 7 system. In this case, it's actually a simpler procedure because you can make sure that the new Windows 7 system is running and configured before you copy your data off the old system. This allows you to run the migration with both systems side by side, and it also gives you the option of going back if you aren't happy with a choice during your migration. You also have the option of performing a live migration, directly from one system to the other.

For this example, we use PC Mover software to demonstrate the process.

caution

You should be aware of an important caveat with regard to the PC Mover software: it is licensed on a per-migration basis. This means that you must pay for *each migration you perform*. This is important because it means that if you buy the Home edition of the PC Mover software, it is licensed for a single migration only—if you run into any issues during the migration that require you to remigrate your system, you will have already used the license and will need to buy another one. Similarly, if you are using the Integrator or Enterprise editions, which come with prelicensed bundles of migrations (20 for Integrator, 20, 100, or 500 for Enterprise), you will pay for each migration attempt.

---

note

PC Mover can be purchased directly from the LapLink Software website:

www.laplink.com/pcmover

Because your PC Mover license covers only one migration (unless you have purchased bundles of migrations for an office setting), this means in practice that you need to preplan your migration, including reading the PC Mover documentation ahead of time and making sure that no issues exist *before* you actually perform the migration. You will not have the option of performing a test migration to troubleshoot any issues, without paying for that test. So *plan ahead.*

In migrating to a new computer, one thing we have found performing direct migration very handy. In the previous section, we discussed using a file-based migration in which your migrated settings and data from your old system installation are stored in a data file and then loaded into the new system. You can use that same approach when moving data from one computer to another, as well, but it is not the approach we recommend.

Instead, we recommend that you create a physical connection between the two computers. Rather than storing the migrated applications, settings, and data files, the connection is used to directly transfer the information to the new computer, where it is immediately installed appropriately.

To perform a direct migration, you need one of the following:

- A USB direct-connect cable. When you purchase the PC Mover software, you can buy a bundled cable for use with the software. Alternatively, you can buy one separately. Note that you need to use the correct type of USB cable—either USB 1.1 or USB 2.0. Although your Windows 7 computer is almost certain to be USB 2.0 capable, if your older computer has a Pentium II-grade CPU, it is probably only USB 1.1 compatible, and you will need to use the USB 1.1 cable. If you are uncertain, be aware that the USB 2.0 cable can be used on a USB 1.1 system, albeit at lower speeds.

- A network connection between the two computers. If you have a network hub/switch (note that these are commonly included in many modern cable modems and DSL routers if you have a broadband connection), or are using a wireless connection, you can directly connect the two computers across the network.

Our preference if at all possible is to use the network connection rather than the USB cable. There are two reasons for this:

- If your old computer uses a high-speed Internet connection, you will presumably be using that same high-speed Internet connection with the new system. Why not take advantage of that connection to perform your migration?

- Frankly, it's faster. Significantly faster. To illustrate, we once performed the same migration using a USB cable and a Fast Ethernet network connection. The migration performed using the USB cable took 14 times as long to perform—16 hours versus 1 hour and 15 minutes over the network.

You also have the option, of course, of migrating using the file method we discussed in the previous section. If that is the case, use that same procedure. When you reach Task 3, however, you should be working on your new computer rather than installing Windows 7 on your old system.

Broadly speaking, when moving apps and data from one computer to another, you will have five tasks to perform:

- Perform premigration setup if you are going to use a network connection.

- Install the migration software on both computers.

- Create a connection between the computers (either USB cable or over the network)

- Use the migration software to perform the migration.

- Clean up.

---

note

As far as we can tell, PC Mover does not support migration of security software. Therefore, this is the one type of software that you must manually install, preferably before you install your other migrated software.

Task 1: Premigration Setup for Network Connect

If you plan to use a network connection to perform your migration, you need to do a small amount of setup first.

1. If you use some form of high-speed Internet connection, make sure that both computers can access the Internet simultaneously. This should involve nothing more than connecting your new computer to the same Internet hub that your old computer is using. If, however, you are using a dial-up connection and you have a local network, you will need to separately attach your computer to your network and configure it, in the same manner that your older computer was connected and configured.

2. Determine the old computer's IP address by selecting the Start menu and selecting All Programs, Accessories, Command prompt. This launches a command prompt window.

3. In the command window, type **ipconfig /all** and press Enter. See Figure 5.14.

Write down the host name, being sure to note that this is for the old PC.

Write down this IP number, being sure to note that this is for the old PC.

FIGURE 5.14

Choose where you want to store your application archive.

4. Write down the number listed next to IP Address. In this case, the number is 192.168.1.113.

5. Scroll up a bit until you can see the Host Name entry. Write down the name listed. In this case, the name is remington.

6. Leave the command prompt window open for the time being.

7. Determine the new computer's IP address, using the same procedure as for finding the old computer's IP. Again, leave the command prompt window open. For this example, our new computer has the IP address 192.168.1.51 and the name Goddess. Write this information down, being sure to note that it is for the new computer.

8. Verify that the old computer can see the new computer on the network. In the command prompt window on the old computer, type **ping** *xxx.xxx.xxx.xxx*, where *xxx.xxx.xxx.xxx* is the IP address of the new computer. You should see a set of messages stating that a reply occurred (as shown in Figure 5.15).

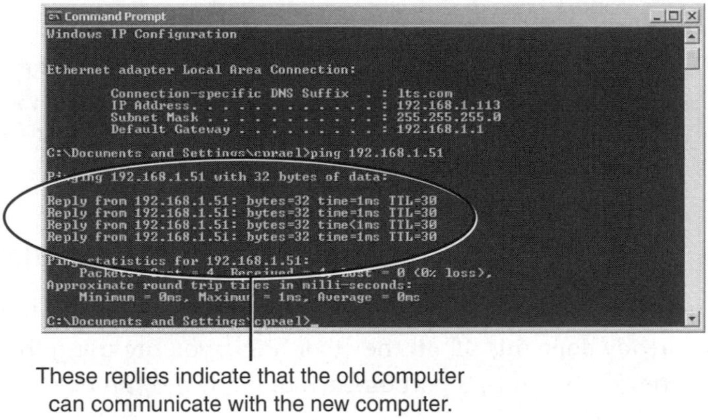

These replies indicate that the old computer
can communicate with the new computer.

FIGURE 5.15

Ping your new computer from the old computer to ensure that the two computers can "see" each other.

9. Verify that the new computer can also see the old computer, using the same procedure as for determining that the old computer can see the new computer.

10. Close the command prompt windows on both computers.

If the two computers can't see each other, you need to diagnose and resolve why that would be the case. One problem that we have seen on occasion is two computers having the same IP address, which would cause an immediate failure. Beyond that, you probably want to call your local computer/networking expert for help resolving the problem, if you don't know how to resolve the problem yourself. Alternatively, a quick search on Google turns up a number of network troubleshooting pages that describe basic steps you can follow to fix your problem.

Task 2: Install the Migration Software

In this case, we assume that you have downloaded the software from the Laplink website. Install the software on both computers. Note that what you are purchasing from Laplink is the migration license. You can download the PC Mover installer software directly from the Laplink website to each computer, if needed, from this web page:

www.laplink.com/pcmover

note

Note that you might need to install the USB driver if you plan to use the USB cable connection for your migration. Preferably, you should be able to use your own system's USB driver. If there is a problem with that, however, download and install Laplink's USB driver for the crossover cable.

Task 3: Create a Connection Between the Two Computers

If you are using a network connection to perform your migration, you have already done this. If, on the other hand, you are using the USB cable, connect it to a USB port on each of the two computers.

Task 4: Use the Migration Software to Perform Your Migration

To perform the migration, follow these steps:

1. Run PC Mover on both computers. Either double-click the PC Mover icon on the desktop or click the Start button and select Programs, PC Mover, PC Mover.

2. To make sure you are running the most recent version of PC Mover, click the Check for Updates button as shown in Figure 5.16. Generally speaking, if you have downloaded the software from the Laplink website, it should be current. Click Next when done.

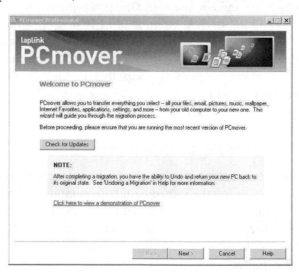

FIGURE 5.16

It's best to check the Laplink website to ensure that you have the most recent version of the PC Mover software.

For the purposes of this section, we're going to bypass the In-Place Upgrade instructions. However, if you are directly upgrading your system from Windows XP to Windows 7, you should turn to the section at the end of the chapter on Using PC Mover to Upgrade from Windows XP to Windows 7.

3. In each running version of PC Mover, specify which computer you are working on. On your original computer, select Old. On your Windows 7 system, select New and then click the Next button on both computers. The screen on the old computer is shown in Figure 5.17.

FIGURE 5.17

Choose where you want to store your application archive.

4. Before you can begin your migration, you must enter your serial number on one of the systems (as shown in Figure 5.18).

note

You can bypass the need for a serial number temporarily by performing a trial migration, that only moves a single type of file. Once you are ready to perform your full migration, however, you must have a valid serial number.

5. You can, however, wait to do so until you have gone through the setup PC Mover requires for your migration. Click the Next button when you are ready to proceed.

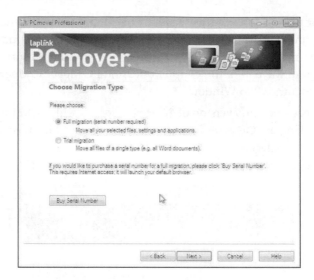

FIGURE 5.18

You may enter your serial number now or later.

      6. Select the transfer method you want to use (see Figure 5.19). If you have connected the USB cable between the two computers, you should see the USB option. In our case, we will use the network connection. Click Over a Network, and then click Next.

FIGURE 5.19

Choose the right kind of transfer method; unless there's a really good reason to use USB, we highly recommend transferring via a network connection.

7. Now you need to arrange the software connection between the two computers. Because PC Mover is running on both your old and new computers, from your old computer, enter the name of your new computer (see Figure 5.20). In this example, we enter "Goddess" as the New Computer Network Name and click Next.

FIGURE 5.20

Here you will set up the software connection between your old and new computers.

8. If for some reason you don't know what the network name is, click the Browse button. This opens a new dialog window allowing you to browse for the new computer (see Figure 5.21).

FIGURE 5.21

You can locate your network by clicking the Browse button.

9. PC Mover displays a Ready to Load screen. Click Next to continue.

10. PC Mover connects to the new computer and determines what new software needs to be loaded for the migration to occur. It does this by building a snapshot view of the configuration of the new computer, as shown in Figure 5.22.

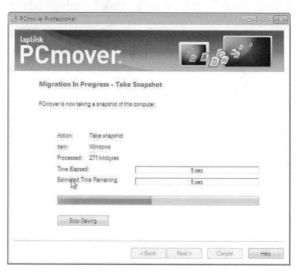

FIGURE 5.22

Building a snapshot.

11. The old computer then looks at that snapshot view and determines what needs to be moved. Based on that, it builds a moving journal, which is a comprehensive list of every file, application, and setting that needs to be moved. You'll have to go through several dialog boxes, with various options to deselect items you do not want to migrate or the ability to add new items that were not selected. Eventaully, you will build a moving journal, detailing everything that needs to be moved, as shown in Figure 5.23.

12. Once you have finished creating the moving van, the two computers will automatically connect and pass off their data, migrating your files from the old computer to the new one.

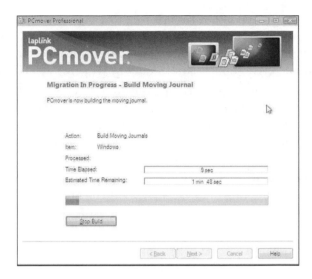

FIGURE 5.23

PC Mover then creates a comprehensive list of every item that will be moved from the old computer to the new computer.

Task 5: Clean Up

Now all you need to do is clean up from your migration. Follow these steps:

1. Uninstall PC Mover from your new computer.
2. Remove and put away the USB cable, if you elected to use one.
3. Shut down and remove your old computer.

Using PC Mover to Upgrade from Windows XP to Windows 7

One surprising finding we ran into while writing this book was that Microsoft has no plans to support a direct upgrade of your computer from Windows XP to Windows 7. Why do we call this surprising? Because Microsoft identified 66 different upgrade scenarios—the various upgrades that they expect their core customers to perform. Yet only 14 of those upgrade scenarios are supported by their own installer. The single biggest set of those upgrade scenarios that they don't support? Migrating from some form of Windows XP to some form of Windows 7.

So when we found out that Laplink had decided to provide support for in-place upgrades in the newest version of their PC Mover software, we were quite delighted. We were even more delighted when we found that PC Mover would even handle some of our old Windows 2000 systems.

So, how do you do an in-place upgrade from Windows XP/2000, using the PC Mover software? It's actually quite simple. PC Mover includes a new Windows Upgrade Assistant mode, which creates a complete repository for your system configuration. Basically, the process is as follows:

1. Download and install PC Mover on your existing Windows computer. One small quirk that we noted in this is that you need to be able to re-install PC Mover after you have upgraded your operating system. We found two ways to do this easily.

    •   Copy the installer to an external storage device of some sort. This could be a CD-ROM, flash drive, or an external hard disk. It might even mean emailing it to yourself (though we had problems with that, too; whether you can do that depends on your email provider, but Google Mail was not friendly to our attempts).

    •   Alternatively, you can hide the installer on your hard disk, where it will be available later (as shown in Figure 5.24). What we did in this case was to open Windows Explorer, create a directory called TEMP on the hard drive, and then copy the installer into that directory.

PC Mover software hidden on the hard drive

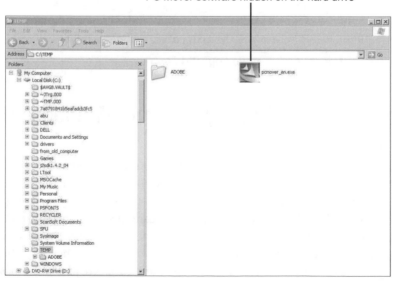

FIGURE 5.24

Hiding the PC Mover installer on your hard disk.

2. Once you have done that, you follow the instructions in the PC Mover In-Place Upgrade documentation, which is available here:

   http://www.laplink.com/pcmover/inplaceupgrade?s=100

   The documentation is in a PDF file, but it completely describes what you need to do, and how to do it, to upgrade your existing Windows 2000 or XP system to a Windows 7 system.

Disposing of Your Old Computer

One issue you need to resolve when you are done with your migration is what to do with your old computer, if you migrated from an old system to a new system. This includes dealing with both the hardware and the software and applications you have installed.

Software Issues

After you have migrated to your new system, remember that the licenses for all of your software migrated as well. In addition, you need to consider the impact of your use on the computer. For example, if you have been buying things online, or doing online banking, you probably have stored passwords and more on the old system. In addition, some software, including many tax preparation packages and financial management software such as Quickbooks, store a variety of your personal financial information on the computer.

At the very least, we recommend uninstalling any software that might be at issue. This includes both licensed software that you migrated and any financial management software that you used.

Our preference, however, is to wipe systems such as this completely, reinstall the operating system, or just delete everything on the hard disk. This ensures that your personal information will not be accidentally passed on to someone else. Contact a computer professional for assistance with this if you have any questions.

Disposing of Your Hardware

After you have migrated to your new system, you may want to dispose of your old computer. We recommend a number of options:

- Sell it to someone else who has a use for it. We've both bought and sold surplus equipment on Craigslist and eBay, and find both places to be vibrant marketplaces.

- Donate your old computer to an entity that can use it, possibly a nonprofit organization or a local school. A quick search online should find someone who can help you with this.

- You can also dispose of it. If you go this route, find your local e-waste recycler. Many cities now have free e-waste recycling programs, some even accept items as donations, allowing you take a modest tax deduction. But if at all possible, avoid disposing of your electronics in the trash; many states now provide criminal penalties for doing so.

6

New Windows 7 Features

Microsoft has gone to great lengths to provide Windows 7 users with
a much more user-friendly interface, along with a number of features users have requested. Vista users will find much that's familiar,
along with some new and some upgraded features. XP users will
find a vastly changed user interface and many new applications
and features (as well as some apps and features that have gone by
the wayside). Further, Windows 7 has been constructed so that
upgrading from one version of Windows 7 to another is relatively
painless.

This chapter explores some of the new features of Windows 7.

---

note

When writing this book, we used Windows 7 Professional, so the new features discussed here are all found in that version of Windows 7. If you use
a different flavor of Windows 7, such as Windows 7 Home Premium, your
mileage might vary. You can see how the different versions of Windows 7
compare by reviewing Table 1.1 in Chapter 1,"Planning Your Upgrade,"
which notes the key feature differences for each of the Windows 7
flavors.

What's on the Desktop

We'll start by examining the items that appear on the Windows 7
desktop when Windows 7 is first installed. However, if you have
already moved things around and customized your version of

Windows 7 (something that Microsoft provides a bevy of ways to do), what appears on your desktop might be different. Also, if you are using a computer purchased from a major PC manufacturer, such as Dell or HP, the items appearing on your desktop will vary as well.

Desktop Background

The desktop background loaded by default could vary, depending on the flavor of Windows 7 installed and whether you purchased your PC from a major manufacturer (such as Dell or HP) with Windows 7 preloaded. As with Windows XP and Vista, you can easily change the background to one of the backgrounds supplied with Windows 7 or use one of your own images. There are literally thousands of free images that you can download from the Web as well.

Clock Gadget

The clock is a Windows gadget that by default is located in the upper-right corner of the desktop (as shown in Figure 6.1). It displays the time in your time zone according to your computer's internal clock. (See more about gadgets later in this chapter.)

Gadget controls

FIGURE 6.1
The clock gadget.

By dragging your mouse over the clock, you'll see a box with three icons to the right of the clock. To close the clock on your desktop, click the X. To reposition the clock, click the clock and drag it to the location you want. To select one of the clock options, click the wrench icon and then choose among the following options:

- **Clock face**—Click the right or left arrows to page through various clock faces.

- **Clock name**—Enter a name for the clock face shown (optional, but useful if you want to have more than one instance of the clock gadget running so that you can see your local time as well as the time in another time zone).

- **Time zone**—The default is the current time zone. Click the down arrow to see a number of other time zones, highlight the one you want to use, and press Enter.

- **Second hand**—Check the box if you want the clock to display the second hand.

note

You can view the gadget control items for any of the gadgets on your desktop (not just the clock) by hovering your mouse over the gadget.

The current digital time and date is also displayed in the lower-right corner of your screen, regardless of whether you have the clock displayed.

View Headlines Gadget

Also on the right side of the screen is the View Headlines gadget, which is another Windows gadget that appears by default (see Figure 6.2).

FIGURE 6.2

The View Headlines gadget requires an active Internet connection and feeds current news headlines right to your desktop.

Many people like to set up their computer to show the latest news headlines. Clicking the arrow in the middle of this icon displays the first few words of the latest headlines on topics about which you've indicated interest. Initially, these are default topics set in the RSS Feeds page on your version of Internet Explorer 8. You can change these topics on the RSS Feeds page when you're using IE8, or you can set that up anytime by clicking the wrench icon and choosing the appropriate option.

Slide Show Gadget

In the lower-right corner is the Slide Show, initially set up with a series of photos from the standard library that comes with Window 7 (see Figure 6.3).

FIGURE 6.3

The slide show gadget lets you to run a series of photos of your choosing, right on your desktop.

You can create your own library of pictures, control how long the picture appears, resize the picture, set or erase transitions between pictures, or shuffle their order with the icons that appear when your cursor hovers over the picture.

Recycle Bin

The Recycle Bin has been a standard feature of various versions of Windows for a long time. It's where you move files or other objects that you want to delete.

Right-click the Recycle
Bin to adjust settings

FIGURE 6.4

Deleted items are stored the Recycle Bin until you permanently delete them.

As with previous versions of Windows, the Recycle Bin is only temporary storage for these items—you also have to right-click the icon and choose Empty Recycle Bin to completely remove the items from your system.

Right-clicking the Recycle Bin and choosing Properties allows you to set the maximum size and to manipulate other controls.

Taskbar

The taskbar is at the bottom of the screen; you use it to launch programs and switch between them when they're open. The taskbar contains icons for programs or directories that have been "pinned" to it or minimized. You can pin any program to the taskbar so it's always just a click away, and you can rearrange the icons on the taskbar just by clicking and dragging. See Figure 6.5.

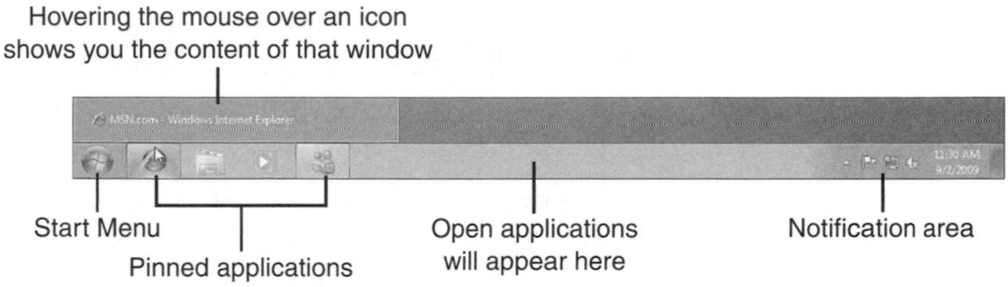

Hovering the mouse over an icon
shows you the content of that window

Start Menu   Open applications   Notification area
          Pinned applications   will appear here

FIGURE 6.5

The icons are bigger than in Vista or XP, so they're easier to use. Hover your cursor over an icon and you'll see a thumbnail of every file or window open in that program. If you hover over that thumbnail, you'll see a full-screen preview of that window.

The default icons that appear in the taskbar are shown in Table 6.1.

Table 6.1   Default Taskbar Icons

Icon	Description
	The Windows icon, which lets you start application programs and utilities, explore the Control Panel, install or modify external devices and printers, connect to networks, and search for files and directories.
	The Internet Explorer icon, which when clicked starts IE and takes you to the home page you specify.
	The Explorer icon, which lets you search for files and directories.
	The Windows Media Player icon, which lets you set up the Media Player and run Internet-based radio, TV, movies, and video.

On the right side of the taskbar are icons for tasks whose screens have been minimized. This area is called the notification area. These icons can include warnings and messages about software updates, security programs, external devices, and so on. The area between the pinned Start menu/pinned application area and the notification area is where open or working application screens will appear.

Changes to the Graphical User Interface

Windows 7 includes some nifty new features that affect how you work with open windows and applications. The following sections outline these changes and will help you make the most of these cool new ways to work with open windows and applications.

Aero Peek

Aero Peek is a feature new to Windows 7 that lets you view the desktop temporarily without minimizing all open windows or applications. This can be useful when you just want a quick look at the desktop and don't want to minimize all the open windows in the process.

Activate the Aero Peek feature by pressing the Windows Key and the spacebar simultaneously; then move your cursor to the far right end of the taskbar. The Aero Peek button looks like a gray bar. When your cursor moves over this button, your current desktop appears, with the currently active screens' borders appearing as faint lines.

Aero Shake

Shaking a single window with your mouse clears away background windows. When you want to focus on the task at hand on a desktop cluttered with windows, use your mouse to grab the window bar of the application you want to work in and shake it back and forth. The rest disappear. Another shake restores the background applications to their former state.

You might find this feature most useful on a touchscreen device. Instead of using your mouse to grab a window, just use your finger to grab the application, and move your finger back and forth quickly.

Aero Snap Screen

The Snap Screen lets you resize any window to half the size of your screen and dock it to the left or right side of the screen. If you drag a window all the way to the left or the right of the screen, Windows 7 displays a "glass" overlay on the desktop. When you let go of the mouse button, the window snaps onto that overlay, which is half the screen's size.

Jump Lists

Jump Lists apply to all taskbar application icons and allows easy access to common tasks related to the corresponding application. When you right-click an icon of an application sitting on the Windows 7 taskbar, a Jump Lists contextual menu displays all the last instances of the application in the taskbar, along with some other frequently used functions (see Figure 6.6).

For example, when you right-click the Internet Explorer 8 (IE8) icon on the taskbar, you see a list of your last visited websites or URLs history. In Microsoft Word or Excel, last opened, accessed, and used documents or files appear. Windows Explorer's Jump Lists shows shortcuts to frequently used folders such as Documents, Music, Pictures, and Videos. Microsoft Paint Jump Lists show lists of recently opened images; Windows Media Player 12 (WMP) Jump Lists show the most recently played songs and music tracks, with direct access to common tasks such as "Play all music shuffled."

FIGURE 6.6

Jump Lists show common tasks related to the item, such as recently visited websites.

Invisible Windows

Move your mouse to the lower-right corner of your screen, and most of your open files become invisible (see Figure 6.7). Don't worry—they're still there. You may, for instance, want them to run in background mode, but not clutter up your desktop while you're working.

To see the invisible windows, click the gray bar at the far-right end of the taskbar. The formerly invisible windows appear.

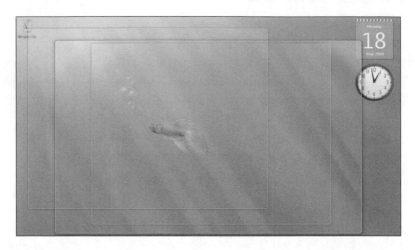

FIGURE 6.7

Move your mouse pointer to the lower-right corner to temporarily hide open windows on your desktop.

Altering Taskbar, Start Menu, and Toolbar Properties

If you right-click the Windows icon, a menu pops up giving you the option of looking at system properties or opening Windows Explorer. Clicking the Properties option lets you change the properties of the taskbar, the Start menu, and toolbars.

Changing Taskbar Properties

If you click the Taskbar tab, you see various options for changing the taskbar (see Figure 6.8).

You can:

- Lock the taskbar in place so that it doesn't move when you change the desktop in other ways.

- Hide the taskbar so that it's always hidden from view. (The default is that the taskbar always appears.)

- Use small icons in the taskbar to indicate which programs and screens are open.

- Move the taskbar to the top, right, or left of the screen. (The default is that the taskbar is at the bottom of the screen.)

FIGURE 6.8
Taskbar properties can be modified in a variety of ways.

- Always or never combine taskbar buttons when more than one instance of a program is open and hide the text labels, or combine only when the taskbar is full.
- Customize the taskbar by moving or resizing it, by selectively turning system, network, Action Center, volume, Windows update, and Family Safety icons on or off, or by always showing all icons and notifications on the taskbar.
- Check how your desktop looks while you're modifying the taskbar.
- Use Aero Peek to preview your desktop.

Changing Start Menu Properties

Likewise, if you click the Start Menu tab, you can set up the Start menu the way you want (see Figure 6.9).

You can:

- Customize how your links, icons, and menus look and behave in the Start menu.
- Set the power button ( ) to shut down, switch users, log off, lock your system, restart, or hibernate.

- Store and display recently opened programs in the Start menu.
- Store and display recently opened items in the Start menu and the taskbar.

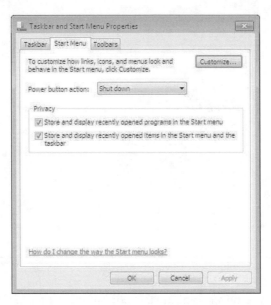

FIGURE 6.9
Modifying the Start menu options.

Changing Toolbar Properties

Finally, you can add toolbars to the taskbar by clicking the Toolbars tab (see Figure 6.10).

You can add the Address, Links, Tablet PC Input Panel, and/or Desktop toolbars to the display area under the primary toolbar.

FIGURE 6.10

Toolbars can be added to the taskbar by clicking the Toolbars tab.

The Calculator

One of the familiar utility programs, the Calculator, has also received a significant upgrade in Windows 7. The default is in the Standard mode, where it operates like a simple four-function calculator. However in Windows 7 there are separate Programmer, Statistics, Unit Conversion, Date Calculation, and Templates modes, similar to the more advanced handheld calculators. More advanced functions in these modes include logarithms; numerical base conversions; logical operations; support for radian, degree, and gradians; and support for simple single-variable statistical functions. We won't cover these in detail in this book, except to say that these modes allow the calculator to operate more as a programmable calculator.

Windows 7 Search Tools

The Windows 7 search program, called Windows Explorer, is launched either by right-clicking the Windows icon in the toolbar or from within Internet Explorer. If you right-click the Windows icon, you can choose the Open Windows Explorer option to open the Explorer window (see Figure 6.11).

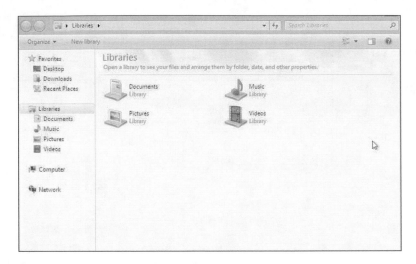

FIGURE 6.11

Information is organized into libraries, which helps speed up locating the item for which you are searching, such as a photo.

In Windows Explorer, information can be organized by libraries, making it easier to find. In the default organization, shown in Figure 6.11, files are organized into documents, music, pictures, and videos, although you can organize your information any way you want.

Windows 7 uses libraries to show all content of a particular type in one spot. By collecting things into a single view, libraries make it simpler to find what you're looking for.

tip

Think of libraries as a collection of shortcuts to files of a similar type. For instance, you might have photos stored in several locations on your hard drive, but with a photo library, shortcuts to each of those locations are gathered in one window.

You can search your libraries using filters to customize your search. For example, when you're looking for music you can search by album. Or you can search for photos by the date they were taken. You can go to your Documents Library, click authors, and see all the documents on your computer sorted by author name. See Figure 6.12.

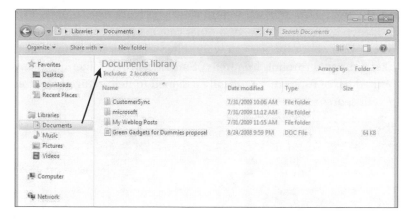

FIGURE 6.12

Libraries are a group of shortcuts that consolidate links to similar kinds of files in one location.

The easiest way to see what you can do with libraries is to click on the Libraries icon. Even if you've just installed Windows 7 and haven't transferred any of your own files, there will probably be several libraries and a couple of files or folders in each. If you click on the Documents library, you'll probably see a couple of files. Clicking on the Organize tab will display the kinds of activities you can perform with a selected library, folder, or file. You can cut, copy, paste, rename, and delete a selected item; change its layout; and change its properties. You can create new libraries and folders. You can choose to share the item with one or more other users, although you'll have to specify what network the other users are on. (You can turn on "network discovery" so that the system can look for the user automatically, if you can't remember the proper path.) You can also burn a copy of a selected library, folder, or file to an external storage device.

Working with libraries is simple:

- To create, change, or delete a library, simply right-click in the Libraries folder.

- To create a new library, right-click an empty space in the Libraries folder, and select New, Library.

- To modify an existing library, right-click the library and select Properties. Make any changes you feel appropriate.

- To delete a library, right-click the library and select Delete. The library will be moved to the Recycle Bin. What's worth noting is that the contents of the library—the individual files—are not deleted.

Search filters make it easier to find what you want (see Figure 6.13). Sort on file type, file size, name, and other categories. If you know any bits of information about the file you want, filter searches can reduce the time it takes to browse through hundreds of matches. Each folder has a customized list of filters automatically assigned to help return better results in your searches.

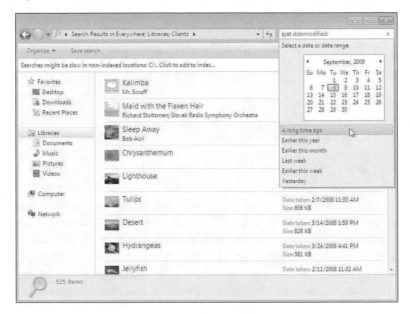

FIGURE 6.13
Using the Date Search filter.

When browsing search results, the Preview pane lets you see a quick preview of the selected documents to help reduce time spent opening and reading documents. The Preview pane makes finding phrases or words in a document easy, too.

Changes to the Control Panel

Big improvements have been made in Windows 7 to device control, performance, the use of virtual hard disks, and other features managed in the Control Panel. Further, many new items have been added to the Control Panel, including the following:

- ClearType Text Tuner
- Gadgets
- Recovery

- Troubleshooting
- Workspaces Center
- Location and Other Sensors
- Credential Manager
- Biometric Devices
- System Icons
- Display

We'll look at some of these and other features in the following sections.

---

note

Not all of the items discussed here are present in all versions of Windows 7.

Device Management

In previous versions of Windows, utilities to control your printer, your scanner, your USB drives, your hard drives, and so on were scattered around the Control Panel. In Windows 7, they're all collected on the Device Manager, shown in Figure 6.14.

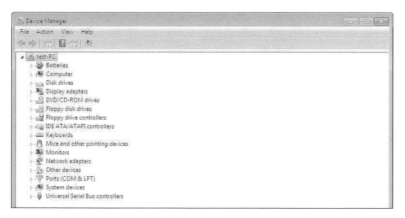

FIGURE 6.14

The Device Manager consolidates controls for scanners, printers, USB drives, hard drives, and more.

Click the triangle at the left of the type of device and you'll get a list of devices connected to your system. Double-click one of them and you'll get a screen where you can see all the applications, services, and information related to your device and where you can manipulate this information, including installing and uninstalling.

Device Manager not only works for devices connected to a Windows 7 PC via USB, but Bluetooth and Wi-Fi as well. In many cases, software installation isn't required for Device Manager—any additional drivers you might need are automatically retrieved the next time you do a Windows Update.

Devices and Printers

Clicking the Devices and Printers item on the right side of the Control Panel takes device management a step further. This screen shows pictures of the devices connected to your system, which makes it really easy to identify what you have installed (see Figure 6.15). This screen also helps you interact with any compatible device connected to your computer. You can see device status and run common tasks from the same window.

FIGURE 6.15

The Device Manager lets you select by picture which device you want to use.

Manufacturers will be able to supply pictures of their devices and APIs for this page. For example, if your camera manufacturer offers a custom version of an API that works with Windows 7, when you plug your camera into your PC you could see information such as the number of photos on your camera and links to helpful information (see Figure 6.16).

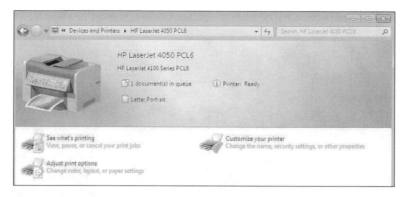

FIGURE 6.16

Custom Device pages provide helpful information not previously found in Device Manager.

Performance

In general, Windows 7 uses less power, takes up less memory, and is more efficient than either Vista or XP. This is particularly noticeable in disk access. If you have two connected PCs, your files will automatically be synchronized between them, making it easier to move files back and forth. This also means that your ability to send streaming media to your cell phone, for instance, will go faster. It also means that your gaming experience will be faster (depending, of course, on your machine).

You'll notice that your PC running Windows 7 will start up, shut down, resume from standby, and respond faster than it did under either Vista or XP.

Power Management

The Power Options selection on the Control Panel lets you set a password when your computer wakes up, choose what the Power button does, and choose a power plan. Power plans can help you save energy when your computer isn't active or maximize your computer's performance.

For instance, adaptive display brightness dims the display if you haven't used your PC for a while (see Figure 6.17). This can save battery life on a laptop.

The default Power Plan balances performance with energy consumption. You can also choose the Power Saver Plan, which saves energy by reducing your computer's performance where possible, or create a customized Power Plan.

Display after it is dimmed   Normal display brightness

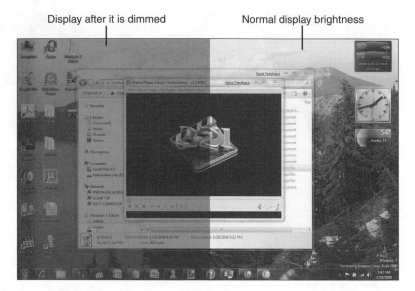

FIGURE 6.17

Adaptive display brightness will dim your display after a certain period of inactivity.

Virtual Hard Disks

A virtual hard disk (VHD) lets multiple operating systems sit on a single host computer and run independently of each other. This means, for instance, that you can run programs on different operating systems without having to switch to different hardware. Among other things, you can

- Move files between a VHD and the host file system.
- Do backup and recovery between systems.
- Take advantage of antivirus and security features in different environments.
- Simultaneously compare an application running in one environment with the same application running in another.
- Create an application file in one environment (for example, a graphic file in an Apple environment) and copy and paste the result into a file in another environment (such as a word processing file running in a PC environment).

For more information on using VHDs within Windows 7, and virtualization in general, see Chapter 11, "Virtualization."

ClearType Text Tuner

Sometimes words on a screen don't appear as sharp as they do when printed on paper. The ClearType Text Tuner is a feature that sharpens the words on your screen to make them easier and sharper to read (see Figure 6.18).

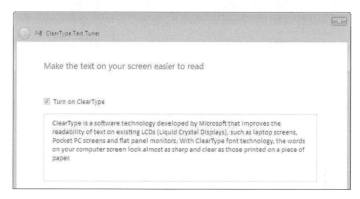

FIGURE 6.18

Turn on the Clear Type option to make your onscreen text easier to read.

When you click the Next button, you see a series of four windows containing text boxes with different versions of text. In each window, select the box with text that looks sharpest to you. After you make your choices, Windows 7 shows you text in the sharpness you wanted. You can then name this text and save it, make it a default, or go back and look at other choices.

Gadgets

Gadgets are simple single-purpose applications, such as a clock, a calendar, a headline feed, or a stock indicator, that can sit on your computer desktop or are hosted on a web page. In Windows 7, the gadgets are located directly on the desktop. They can also be used to control external applications such as Windows Media Center.

Ten default gadgets come installed: Calendar, Clock, CPU Meter, Currency, Feed Headlines, Media Center, Picture Puzzle, Slide Show, Stocks, and Weather Gadgets are usually aligned on either side of the screen, but can also be placed elsewhere on the screen.

You can access the current set of gadgets in the Control Panel by clicking the Desktop Gadgets icon. This displays a set of gadgets and lets you page through the currently installed gadgets (see Figure 6.19).

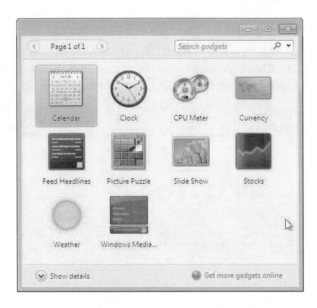

FIGURE 6.19

Ten gadgets come installed on Windows 7, though there are many more that you can freely download.

Double-clicking the icon for a particular gadget causes it to appear on your desktop. (To remove it, click the X in the bar to the right of the gadget.)

You can also see the set of gadgets by right-clicking anywhere on the desktop and, in the drop-down menu, selecting Gadgets, as shown in Figure 6.20.

FIGURE 6.20

Getting the gadgets installed on your computer is easy—right-click the desktop and choose— you guessed it—Gadgets.

Sticky Notes

The Notes gadget that appeared in Vista has been replaced it with a program called Sticky Notes, accessed from the Start window. If you're like a lot of users who scribble notes on Post-Its® and attach them to your screen or on the edges of your monitor, you'll love Sticky Notes.

You create a Sticky Note by clicking the Start button and selecting Sticky Notes on the menu that appears (see Figure 6.21).

FIGURE 6.21

Sticky Notes allow you to create notes on your desktop to help you remember important bits of information.

You can expand the size of the Sticky Note or close it by clicking the controls. If you're working on an application that uses your entire screen, and you minimize it to see your desktop, the Sticky Notes will not appear, however.

Recovery

Windows Recovery Environment (Windows RE) is a combination runtime environment, diagnostic tool, and repair system that basically tries to do about 80% of what the engineers in the Windows support team could do if they came to your home or office and hooked up a debugger up to your PC—all without you having to do much.

If your system runs into problems, you can start Windows Recovery Environment by booting from the CD, and then choosing to repair your computer (see Figure 6.22). Once you identify the operating system to repair, you'll be presented with a number of options.

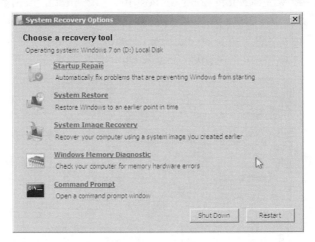

FIGURE 6.22

The Windows Recovery Environment will help you diagnose and fix problems.

Some of these options assume a fairly high level of technical expertise, or of prior planning. The System Image Recovery option, for example, requires that you have previously backed up your system in order to create the system image you would use for recovery.

Generally speaking, you will find Startup Repair and System Restore to be the most important tools. Beyond that point, we strongly suggest that you contact an experienced computer technician.

Troubleshooting

One of the most common problems users have with Microsoft software is what happens when your computer crashes and you don't know what to do. Many have experienced the frustration of calling Microsoft's Help number and waiting for what seems like forever to talk to someone who can help.

The Troubleshooting screen, available from the Control Panel, walks you through many troubleshooting scenarios so that you are likely to be able to solve your problem on your own, without waiting on hold for someone to pick up the phone.

When the screen first appears, you'll be asked if you want the most up-to-date content available. Click Yes to update the library of troubleshooting scenarios and tips. Proceed to select either troubleshooting programs for previous versions of Windows or the type of problem you're having (see Figure 6.23).

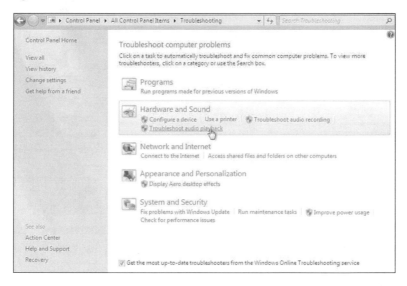

FIGURE 6.23

The Troubleshooting tool is your first stop when things aren't working as planned.

The troubleshooting scenarios are organized as trees, with each successive screen giving you more suggestions and resources particular to your problem, most starting with directing you to built-in Help and Support files that may help with solutions.

Workspaces Center

Many people share their computer's resources through a concept called a *workspace*. This means that certain resources on your computer are available to other team members currently in the workspace. Using Microsoft Office Live under Windows 7, you can make all your computer's resources available to other team members (see Figure 6.24).

FIGURE 6.24

Workspaces allow you to create a common working area for multiple people in different locations.

Location and Other Sensors

You can set up your Windows 7 environment so that your computer and applications adapt to the current environment. Location sensors, including GPS devices, WWAN radios, and triangulation devices, will know exactly where they are, enabling them to provide more locally relevant content and functionality. (Think of the location technology illustrated in the current crop of police dramas on TV, for instance. You could have the same technology enabled, for instance, on a cell phone or PDA that is connected to your PC.)

Ambient light sensors, for example, can allow your computer to automatically adjust your screen's brightness based on the current lighting conditions. They can also allow applications to optimize their content for readability, making your computer more useful in a range of operating environments.

To set up or control these sensors, choose the Location and Other Sensors option on the Control Panel. Your screen will display the set of sensors currently installed. Choose one and you can view the activity reported by that sensor. A menu bar on the right lets you perform a number of actions on the data, including setting up filters.

Credentials Manager

Older versions of Windows allowed you to set cookies or other automated procedures that let you quickly log in to password-protected websites and use private documents and other files. With Windows 7 you can use the Credentials Manager, an item on the Control Panel, to store your user IDs and passwords safely in the Windows Vault, where they can't be retrieved by keystroke capture programs or other spyware.

Windows Vault stores these credentials so that, when needed, Windows can use them to log in a user automatically to a website or another computer. This means that any Windows application that needs credentials to access a resource (server or a website) can make use of the Credentials Manager and Windows Vault and use the credentials supplied instead of prompting the user to enter a user ID and password each time. See Figure 6.25.

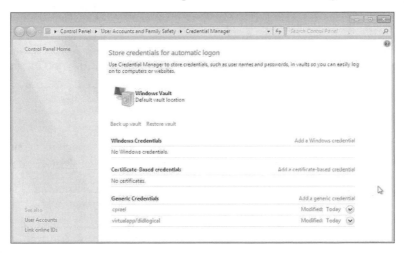

FIGURE 6.25

Credentials Manager keeps your login information for several sites in one handy place.

What's new in Windows 7, however, is the capability to back up and restore the Vault, such as to a USB thumb drive, so that a user's security can be protected.

Biometrics

In previous versions of Windows, biometric authentication and management of biometric devices (for example, fingerprint sensors) required third-party software that sometimes didn't work well with Windows. Now it's built in. Windows 7 includes the Windows Biometric Framework, an API developers can use to build biometrics into applications.

Biometric devices are managed through a Control Panel applet, shown in Figure 6.26.

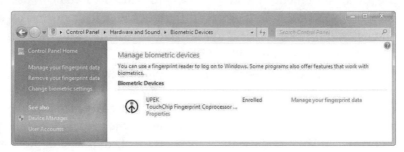

FIGURE 6.26

Biometric controls are built in to Windows 7 instead of being add-ins that might not work properly, as was the case with previous editions of Windows.

This allows more fingerprint sensors on networked computers, increasing the security level.

Networking

Windows 7 offers a simpler network interface than in previous versions, more home-user features, and has redesigned certain basic networking functions to make them easier to use. You can quickly see how your network is configured by clicking the Network and Sharing Center item on the Control Panel (see Figure 6.27).

Here you can set up a new connection or a new network; connect to a wired, wireless, dial-up, or VPN connection; configure your home group; and troubleshoot your network problems. You can also tweak your Internet connections and your Windows firewall. System and network security is covered in more detail later in this chapter and in Chapter 8, "Windows Security."

This section briefly looks at the new Windows networking environment. For a more detailed examination, however, including configuring Windows 7 networking with your existing network devices, see Chapter 9, "Windows Networking."

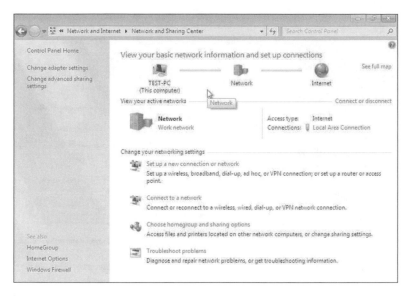

FIGURE 6.27

Access the simplified networking interface via the Network and Sharing Center.

HomeGroups

By far the biggest change to Windows networking is Windows 7's use of the HomeGroup. If you're running Windows 7 at home or in a small office, you probably need to share an Internet connection and possibly devices such as a printer, a scanner, and maybe access to files. Or you might need to find a file but don't know which computer it's stored on.

Previously, you might have bought an off-the-shelf package that you then used to connect your computers and devices, and you probably spent hours setting up your network, dealing with security issues, and configuring it all. It's all in one place in Windows 7.

HomeGroup makes connecting the computers in your home a painless process. Windows 7 automatically sets it up when you add the first PC running Windows 7 to your home network. You can specify exactly what you want to share from each PC with all the PCs in the HomeGroup. You and your daughter can use the same printer from anywhere on the network. You can store digital photos on a computer at home and easily get them from a laptop connected wirelessly to your HomeGroup. Your son can listen to music at school on his cell phone connected to your network at home.

Start by choosing the HomeGroup item on the Control Panel, as shown in Figure 6.28.

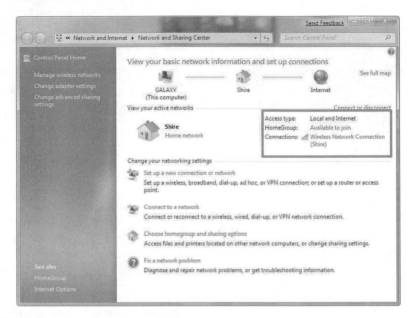

FIGURE 6.28

The HomeGroup option automatically creates a HomeGroup for you and invites you to join. The HomeGroup is marked in this figure.

When you click one of the devices under HomeGroup, you'll see the types of libraries available on that device (see Figure 6.29). Clicking any icon lets you explore the contents of that library.

FIGURE 6.29

The bars to the right show you which libraries are currently available.

Click the Network icon to see what's available on your network, as shown in Figure 6.30. Highlighting one of the networks and clicking the Connect button seamlessly connects you to that network.

FIGURE 6.30

You can find your folders and files by clicking on their names.

Wireless Networking

Connecting to new wireless networks is something that has been made significantly easier in Windows 7. In the taskbar's notifications tray, clicking the wireless signal icon brings up a list of available networks around you. You can connect to an unsecure network or enter in your security code on a secure network and click the Connect button. Disconnecting is just as easy. To learn more about wireless networking with Windows 7, see Chapter 9, "Windows 7 Wireless Networking."

Direct Access

DirectAccess keeps users connected to the corporate network whenever they are online—without the use of a virtual private network (VPN). This is particularly appealing to IT managers: they can better manage remote workers who will be connected to the network more frequently and be available for security patches and software updates.

BranchCache

BranchCache speeds up access to remote files for workers in branch offices by caching a copy of files locally after the workers access them from the corporate network. The BranchCache feature comes in two forms: a local cache hosted on the server or on branch PCs running Windows 7 directly.

Security (Windows Action Center)

Security for your computer is now managed via the Windows Action Center (previously called the Windows Security Center), which lets users view the status of computer security settings and services. It continually monitors these security settings and informs the user via a pop-up notification balloon if a problem occurs.

The Windows Action Center has three major components: a control panel, Windows Service, and an application programming interface (API).

Windows Action Center Control Panel

The control panel (see Figure 6.31) displays the monitored security settings into categories; bars for the categories are displayed with a background color of light blue, yellow, or red. A category with a blue background indicates that the settings in the category are healthy. A yellow background typically indicates that some or all of the settings in that category are not being monitored. A red background indicates a problem that can expose the user's computer to problems.

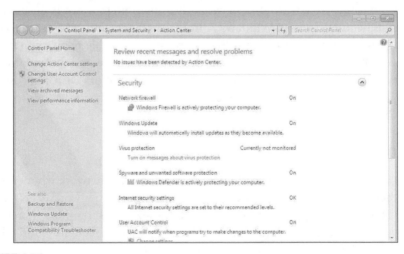

FIGURE 6.31

The Windows Action Center tracks important settings and alerts you when you need to take action.

Windows Service

The current state of these settings is determined by the Windows Service via the Windows Security Center (see Figure 6.32). This service starts automatically when the computer starts, continually monitoring the system for changes and informing the user via a pop-up box a problem exists.

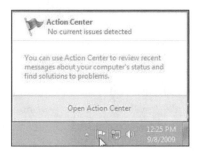

FIGURE 6.32

Windows Service is loaded at startup and continually monitors the system.

APIs

The primary interface that third-party antivirus, anti-malware, and firewall software vendors use to register with Windows Security Center is through the WMI provider. APIs are available that can be used by any application that wants to confirm that the system is in a healthy state before engaging in certain actions. For example, a computer game may want to ensure that a firewall is running before connecting to a multiplayer online game.

Changes to AutoPlay

Windows 7 no longer displays the AutoRun task in the AutoPlay dialog box except for removable optical media such as CDs and DVDs. In 2007 and 2008, there were numerous reports of malware—notably the Conficker virus—spreading from computer to computer via removable USB thumb disks and other removable media, and therefore this capability was removed.

BitLocker

This feature secures data on USB thumb drives and other external devices. With BitLocker To Go, access to data on removable storage can be restricted to authorized users only through pass phrases set by system administrators.

AppLocker

The AppLocker reduces the threat of users running unauthorized software that could lead to malware infections. It allows system administrators to specify through a Group Policy what exactly is allowed to run on their systems, giving users the confidence that the applications and programs they are running have been granted permission.

Windows Media Center

If you haven't discovered the convenience of watching TV and movies on your computer, or of having your computer control what's displayed on your huge flat-screen TV, welcome to the new age of media. Starting with Vista, Microsoft enabled a digital media player that lets you download, edit, rearrange, and watch photos, videos, or movies, or listen to recorded music and commercial radio. Some users no longer subscribe to cable or satellite TV and simply watch TV via their computers.

With a simple USB TV Tuner you can record and watch shows on your schedule. Windows Media Center has been updated to manage a single TV guide containing both standard and digital high-definition TV shows (see Figure 6.33).

FIGURE 6.33
Windows Media Center allows you to record and watch television shows when you want to watch them, not just when they're aired.

You start the Media Player by clicking the Media Player icon in the taskbar. The first time you do this, you'll be asked to set up the Windows Media

Player, which may take some time. After it is set up, clicking this icon displays a list of frequently accessed sections of Media Center. This can be either specific files, such as photos and videos, or functions, such as TV.

You can toggle back and forth between full screen and minimized modes by clicking anywhere on the content that is playing. Or you can click the View Full Screen icon on the right side of the media controls.

To view your full Media Library along with the interface for managing it, click the Switch To Library icon on the right side of the media controls. After you switch to the Library View, you get the full screen for managing your library.

In Figure 6.34, the primary categories in your digital media library are on the left, what's currently playing is minimized on the right side, and the controls for what's playing are in the bar at the bottom.

FIGURE 6.34

A sample digital media library as viewed with Windows Media Center.

After you pick a category, you'll be able to find your favorite shows quickly with new features such as turbo scroll. Just hold down the right-arrow key and you'll zip through content listings.

Windows 7 now supports many types of media files, including:

- .asf
- .wma

- .wmv
- .wm
- metafiles (.asx, .wax, .wvx, .wpl)
- Microsoft Digital Video Recording (.dvr-ms)
- .wmd
- .avi
- MPG-type files (.mpg, .mpeg, .m1v, .mp2, .mp3, .mpa, .mpe, .mpv2, and .m3u)

In addition, Windows 7 supports .aac audio files and H.264, DivX, and Xvid video files, with no third-party download needed.

Play To

You can use the Windows 7 Media Player to send video or audio to other Windows 7 PCs and DLNA (Digital Living Network Alliance)-certified digital media rendering devices via the Play To feature. With Play To, you can browse or search from within Windows Media Player or Windows Explorer to find the media you want and then choose where you want it to be played. A remote control window appears for each Play To session, giving you the ability to control the entire experience (see Figure 6.35).

FIGURE 6.35

Use the Play To feature to send what would normally appear on your screen to some other device, such as a big screen TV set in the family room.

You can also Play To a cell phone, provided it is DLNA-certified and supports Windows 7. After you've set up the Windows Media Player to stream media to the cell phone, you can select media items to play on a cell phone or another PC. A Play To remote control window appears on the cell phone, providing standard controls like play, pause, stop, skip forward and backward, seek forward and backward, volume, and mute. After the Play To remote control window appears on your cell phone, you can reorder or delete items, add to the queue, or toggle repeat. You can even add new media items from Windows Media Player or Windows Explorer by dragging them into this window.

Streaming Media

Streaming media is pictures, audio, video, or other media that is constantly received by a user while it is being delivered by a streaming provider. Microsoft has been providing support for streaming media since the 1980s, although there have been problems with bandwidth and computers powerful enough to handle that much data that fast. Windows XP and Vista provided some support for streaming media; Windows 7 provides much better support.

In Windows 7, media streaming is enabled and works by default. Configuring media streaming is easy. The Stream menu in the Windows Media Player user interface (see Figure 6.36) lets you do the following:

- Set up your home PC so you can access your media libraries while away from home.
- Allow other Windows 7 PCs and devices to push media to your player and control it.
- Quickly authorize all home PCs and devices to access your media collection.

But after you have the Windows Media Player configured to allow streaming media anywhere in your house (or office), why stop there? If your pictures, music, videos, and recorded TV content are available on your home PC, you take it with you, for example, on a family vacation. You don't have to download what you want onto your laptop or other media player. You can tap into the entertainment on your home PC from pretty much wherever you can connect to the Internet. Use Windows Media Player on your laptop to listen to music and view pictures, videos, or recorded TV in the media libraries on your home PC (see Figure 6.37).

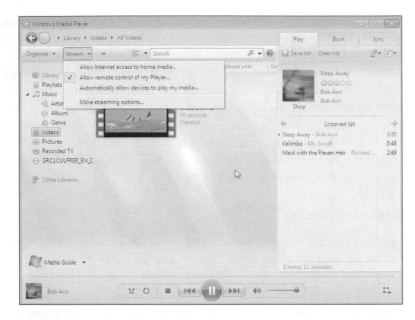

FIGURE 6.36

Use media streaming to access your media while you're way from home, among other things.

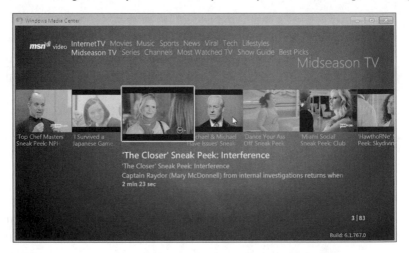

FIGURE 6.37

Yes, you can watch your favorite TV show on your computer! Movies, too!

Windows Live

Windows Live helps synchronize all the ways you communicate and share things online—by giving you one place to go to chat, email, share photos and files you've created, and stay connected with the people and things that matter to you. Figure 6.38 shows Windows Live Photo Gallery.

FIGURE 6.38

Windows Live Photo Gallery.

Under Windows 7, the Windows Live Mail, Windows Live Photo Gallery, and Windows Live Movie Maker programs delivers email, contacts, calendar, and photo and movie-making functionality for Windows from any computer or web-enabled phone. Since these programs and services are delivered online, it's easier to keep them up-to-date and use the latest features.

User Interface Enhancements

Windows 7 has made a variety of improvements to the user interface. We've covered some of the key enhancements here.

Touchscreens

Although great for a lot of tasks, using a keyboard and mouse is not always the easiest way to do things. With Windows 7, if you've got a touchscreen monitor, you can touch your computer screen for a more direct and natural way to work. Use your fingers to scroll, resize windows, play media, and pan and zoom.

The Start menu, Windows taskbar, and Windows Explorer are touch friendly, with larger icons that are easier to select with your finger. Browsing the Web with Internet Explorer 8 is easier, too—just use your finger to scroll down a web page or browse your favorite links. You can even use your finger to arrange the pictures in a photo album.

Windows 7 also introduces support for new multitouch technology, so you can control what happens on the screen with more than one finger. For example, you can zoom in on an image by moving two fingers closer together, like you're pinching something, or zoom out by moving two fingers apart. You can rotate an image on the screen by rotating one finger around another and can right-click by holding one finger on your target and tapping the screen with a second finger. See Figure 6.39.

FIGURE 6.39

Tablet PC functionality has been built in to Windows 7.

Windows 7 upgrades the capability of a Tablet PC to recognize handwriting, including

- Support for handwriting recognition, personalization, and text prediction in new languages
- Support for handwritten math expressions
- Personalized custom dictionaries for handwriting recognition
- New integration capabilities for software developers

Windows Vista supported handwriting recognition for 12 languages: English, German, French, Spanish, Italian, Dutch, Brazilian Portuguese, Japanese, Chinese (Simplified and Traditional), and Korean. For Windows 7, 14 additional languages are supported: Norwegian (Bokmål and Nynorsk), Swedish, Finnish, Danish, Polish, Portuguese (Portugal), Romanian, Serbian (Cyrillic and Latin), Catalan, Russian, Czech, and Croatian.

Remember the Babel fish, the fictitious species in Douglas Adams' *The Hitchhiker's Guide to the Galaxy*? Its utility was to simultaneously translate from one spoken language to another. Yahoo's Babel Fish utility does the same thing with text you type. And now Windows 7 users can launch the Tablet Input Panel (TIP); write in a desired language (for which a recognizer is available); and insert the converted, recognized text into applications such as Microsoft Outlook or Word.

Speech Recognition

Windows Vista had fully integrated support for speech recognition, but it was somewhat buggy and users griped about its performance. In Windows 7, some of those bugs have been resolved. However, the big improvement is that users can now download an updated Speech Recognition Profile Tool that can be used to back up and restore speech profiles created under Vista or on other computers, or when using complex speech profiles.

You can set up your Speech Recognition device (you'll need a microphone or some other audio input device) via the Speech Recognition item on the Control Panel. The same screen walks you through the Speech Tutorial, where the system learns your voice and vocabulary and then offers you tips on helping the system better understand you.

Internet Explorer 8

Windows 7 comes complete with a new version of Internet Explorer—IE8—which has more and better browsing and productivity features than other browsers. Through IE8, you'll also better be able to perform searches across local and networked corporate data, for instance, and better find web-based applications and documents.

Through Windows Media, you'll be able to access streaming online video and audio, turning your computer into traffic director for all your home's picture, audio, video, and movie needs and allowing you to stream media to your cell phone, your friends' or co-workers' computers, or other destinations.

New Features in Internet Explorer 8

IE8 has better tab handling, a new search bar, a more useful address bar, and new tools that deliver information directly from other web pages and services. IE8 has also been tweaked for security and includes new antimalware protection and better ways to protect your privacy.

For basic browsing, the biggest improvement in IE8 is color-coded and grouped tab handling. When you open a new tab on an existing page, the new one opens directly to the right of the originating one, and both tabs have the same color. That way, all related tabs are automatically grouped and color coded so that you don't have to keep track of which tab is related to which page.

It's easy to move a tab between groups—just drag it and it becomes part of the new group, taking on its color. Right-click any tab to control its entire group; that includes closing the group, closing all tabs except for those in the group, and ungrouping the chosen tab from the group. You can also perform actions on any individual tab from the right-click menu.

The new address bar is no longer just a location for typing in a web address. With IE8, when you type something it becomes a search tool that searches previously visited websites, Favorites, and RSS feeds, as well as the entire Web.

Type in a term, and Internet Explorer does a search, using your default search engine. Start to type a URL, and you'll get a list of results from your History and Favorites, organized by category. So, for example, type "gra" and you'll see a list of all of the sites in your History and Favorites that contain those letters—not just at the beginning of the URL, but also in page titles or anywhere in the URL. To visit the site, highlight it in the list and press Enter.

Visual Search

To start, as you type a search request you'll immediately start seeing relevant suggestions from your chosen search provider, complete with images when available. The twist: Search will also use your browsing history to narrow the suggestions. If you see what you're looking for, you can go right to the list without finishing the request.

Under Internet Explorer 8, you also get visual search images that provide you with immediate answers. For example, typing "San Francisco weather" with Live Search will instantly show you a preview of the current Bay Area weather directly in the Search Box drop-down (see Figure 6.40).

FIGURE 6.40

Visual search images help provide you with on-the-spot answers when using Internet Explorer 8.

Using Internet Explorer's Instant Search

That actor in the movie you watched last night—what was his name? Or the full name of Stephen Hawking's book about the universe—what was the title again? Whereas Windows Explorer lets you search for items on your computer, Internet Explorer 8 lets you search the Web and offers relevant suggestions as you type to help save time. Click a suggestion anytime to immediately execute the search without having to type the entire word or phrase.

For instance, if you start typing "Isaac Newton," you might see the results shown in Figure 6.41.

FIGURE 6.41

Instant Search helps find answers fast.

Accelerators

There are online services you use all the time to do simple things, such as mapping a location. With Accelerators, you can highlight a bit of information on any page, click the blue Accelerators icon, and choose from a variety of relevant services. For instance, if you highlight a street address and right-click the mouse, the Live Maps Accelerator will show a preview of the map for that vicinity (see Figure 6.42). In addition to mapping, Windows 7 has Accelerators for emailing, blogging, searching, translating, and sharing information. Popular services including eBay and Facebook offer special Accelerators you can use with their sites.

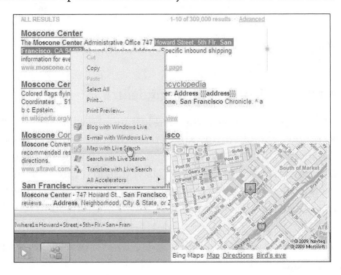

FIGURE 6.42

Highlighting a street address and right-clicking it will show a preview of a map of that vicinity.

IE8's Accelerators speed up your browsing tasks by taking your search directly to action. After you select a bit of text and click the blue icon, you can get driving directions, perform searches, translate or define words, and more, depending on the Accelerators you've installed. IE8 comes with a number of useful Accelerators, but you can add more by going to the Internet Explorer Gallery and customizing your browser with Accelerators from Live Search, eBay, Yahoo!, Wikipedia, Amazon, Facebook, and other sites.

Web Slices

A Web Slice is something you use when you need to track information on a website, but you don't want to keep going to the site (see Figure 6.43).

You instantly see changes on the website without going to it. You can subscribe to specific content within a page and monitor things such as auction items, stock prices, sports scores, entertainment columns, and weather reports. IE8 delivers updated information directly to a Web Slice in your Favorites bar, without leaving the page you're on.

FIGURE 6.43

Web Slices enable you to keep track of changing information on frequently visited sites without actually visiting the site.

When you visit a web page that can deliver information via a Web Slice, the Web Slice icon on the Favorites bar turns green. Click its down arrow and you'll see a list of all Web Slices on the page. Select one, and a listing for the Web Slice then appears on your Favorites bar. When its content changes, the title turns bold. Click the Web Slice, and it drops down and displays the content. You can click through to go to the web page that hosts the slice or view it in the drop-down.

7

New Windows 7 Applications

What's the difference between a new application and a new feature? For this book, we decided that changes to applications that already appeared in Windows XP or Vista, and functionality that's built in to Windows, are *features*, whereas totally new functions and groupings of functions, especially those that you launch and interact with directly, are *applications*. This chapter will be about applications that are new in Windows 7. For that reason, this chapter discusses applications such as Live Essentials and its components and Windows Media Center but doesn't discuss Calculator and Paint, which both have new features. Changes to the taskbar are considered features and were covered in some detail in Chapter 6, "New Windows 7 Features."

Windows Live

Some of the applications that used to be bundled with Windows Vista are now available within the separately downloadable package called Windows Live (www.windowslive.com). Among other things, previous Windows users may have had Windows Messenger, MSN Messenger, and Windows Live Messenger installed simultaneously under Windows XP or Vista. Windows Live Messenger handles those functions now. Further, Microsoft says that it will release and update the programs within Windows Live separately from updates to Windows 7.

note

The new Windows Live represents a shift by Microsoft into the area of cloud computing, according to many observers. Cloud computing uses externally located (usually), dynamically scalable resources (such as large file and network servers) as a service over the Internet. This means that customers do not have to own the physical infrastructure serving as host to the software platform in question. Instead, they rent usage of those resources from some third-party provider. They use those resources as a service and pay only for resources that they use.

As such, there are now three parts to the platform: Windows 7 Core OS, Windows Live applications (bundled together as Windows Live Essentials), and Windows Live Services (Hotmail, Spaces, and so on). Some hardware vendors might even preinstall Windows Live Essentials.

note

Shortly before this book went to print, Microsoft announced that it would merge Windows Live and Office Live into an integrated set of services at one single destination. Windows Live, is a set of software and services that provide mail, instant messaging, blogging and social-networking services. Office Live is a collection of services designed for small businesses and includes Office Live Workspace, Office Live Small Business, and Office Live Groove.

The following are specific applications in Windows Live Essentials:

- Bing (Microsoft's new search engine)
- Windows Live Messenger
- Windows Live Mail
- Windows Live Photo Gallery
- Windows Live Writer
- Windows Live Toolbar
- Windows Live Family Safety
- Windows Live Movie Maker
- Microsoft Office Outlook Connector 12.1
- Windows Live Sync (integrated with Toolbar and Photo Gallery)
- Microsoft Sky Drive
- Microsoft Silverlight

note

Access to any of the Windows Live applications requires that you have a Windows Live ID. You can also use a Passport ID or a Messenger ID. If you don't already have one, you'll be asked to sign up.

Bing

Bing is Microsoft's new search engine. It's enabled as the search facility within Windows Live and lets you perform searches on words, images, video, shopping, news, maps, and travel. Announced in May 2009, it replaced both Microsoft's Live Search and Yahoo's search engine and now includes a listing of search suggestions in real time as queries are entered, along with a list of related searches.

Some of its features include:

- A background image that changes daily. Standard images are of notable places in the world; you can see background information about the image by moving your mouse over the image.

- Separate sections for wallpaper, maps, weather, fan sites, and so on.

- A navigation pan on the left side; results pages display related and prior searches.

- An extended preview on the right side that gives a bigger view of the page and provides links inside of the page.

- Video thumbnail previews that automatically start playing when you hover your mouse over a video thumbnail.

- Image searches with a continuous scrolling image results page that can be adjusted for size, layout, color, style, and people.

- Video searches with adjustable settings for length, screen size, resolution, and source.

- Instant answers for:

  - Sports scores (by specific day, by league, by team, by player).

  - Finance (by entering the stock symbol and either "stock" or "quote" in the search box; Bing provides a subscribable Web Slice that has information such as a stock charts, prices, volumes, and p/e ratios).

  - Math calculations.

  - Package tracking and tracing (by entering the shipping company and tracking number in the search box).

  - Plane ticket price information (by entering the departing flight number with a city name or airport code in the search box).

  - Flight status (by entering "flight status" and a flight number in the search box).

  - Car information.

- Celebrity rankings and news.

- Answers to encyclopedia questions (using the Encarta encyclopedia).

- Dictionary definitions.

- Spell checking.

- Best match (plus similar sites).

- Product shopping and Bing Cashback offers.

- Health information.

- Access to local information, such as:

  - Current traffic.

  - Business listings.

  - People listings.

  - Collections.

  - Local restaurants and services.

  - Restaurant reviews.

  - Movies being showing in a local area. You can also specify a city and the search will provide listings from that area.

  - Hotel listings by city, with maps and a detail search page that lets you see reviews and directions, make reservations, and see a bird's-eye view of the hotel. You can refine your hotel search by rating, price, amenities, payment methods, and parking.

Windows Live Messenger

Messenger (see Figure 7.1) lets you know if you have email and lets you go directly to Hotmail, and to Windows Live Mail if you have it installed. It also lets you know what your friends (those in your Contacts list) are doing via the "What's New" area at the bottom of the page. You can expand the "What's New" area to include new photos and other details.

Messenger also lets you type a personal message at the bottom of your Contacts list and send it, similar to using an Instant Message or Twitter to send a quick message to all of your contacts.

You can also change the layout of your Contacts list and the size and shape of icons representing your contacts.

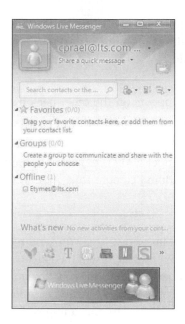

FIGURE 7.1

Stay in touch with friends via Windows Live Messenger.

1. Click the Layout icon; then choose Layout from the menu.
2. Choose the size of your icons and move your categories around as needed.
3. Click the Preview button to see what it will look like. If you like what you see, click OK.

You can also customize your Windows Live Messenger background to suit your current mood.

1. Move your mouse over the upper-right corner of the Contacts pane until the paintbrush appears, and then click it.
2. Scroll through the scenes and select the one you want.
3. Click Apply to see a preview, and click OK to choose it as the background. Your friends will see your new background, too.

Interoperability Between Live Messenger and Yahoo! Messenger

Yahoo! Messenger and Windows Live Messenger users can chat with each other without needing to create an account on the other service, provided both contacts use the latest versions of their respective software.

From either Yahoo! Messenger or Live Messenger, make sure the person you want to talk with is in your Contacts list; then create a message as you normally would.

Zing!

Your message now appears on the other person's screen.

If the other person is using older or third-party software, that user will appear offline to you.

Windows Live Messenger 2009 is expected to improve multiclient support in the near future, adding Google Talk, AOL, ICQ, and XMPP.

Offline Messaging

With Windows Live Messenger, you can send messages to another user who is offline, and the messages will be delivered when that person is logged in to Messenger. In addition, you can start a conversation even when your status is set to Appear Offline (similar to behavior in Yahoo! Messenger and ICQ). If you are messaging with someone who has an older version of MSN Messenger, the other person will lose the ability to talk to you after a short period of no activity because their messaging program will conclude that you are offline.

Windows Live Call

In previous versions of Windows, you could make PC-to-PC phone calls using Voice over Internet Protocol (VoIP). In Windows 7, you can also make PC-to-phone calls with Windows Live Call, as part of Live Messenger.

In the United States, this feature is supported by Telefonica. Orange also has a similar service in France, the United Kingdom, Germany, the Netherlands, Austria, Ireland, Finland, Belgium, Spain, and Italy.

Games and Applications

You can play games or share applications via Windows Live Messenger. Click the Games icon and a window opens, allowing you to challenge your friend or contact to participate in a competition or a game or invite them to launch a shared external application.

The Symbian60 Platform

You can run the S60 version of Windows Live Messenger on mobile phones such as the Nokia Smartphone and others. When enabled, this version includes grouped contacts, voice clips, image and file sending, as well as features unique to S60, such as tabbed chat windows and integration with the contact list and other features of the S60 platform.

When you log on to Windows Live Messenger, you'll be prompted to start the S60 version if it is enabled.

Communicating with an Xbox User

You can use your Xbox 360 console and Xbox Live to connect to your existing Windows Live Messenger contacts and chat as you play a game, watch a movie, or enjoy any other Xbox 360 activity. If you have an Xbox 360 Chatpad, you can also use the Chatpad for easy access to messenger features. To start or respond to conversations from an Xbox 360, follow these steps:

1. Sign in to Xbox LIVE.
2. Press the Xbox 360 Guide button, and then select Chat & IM.

note

You can also press the Messenger icon on your Xbox 360 Chatpad.

3. Select Sign In. When you are prompted, enter your Windows Live ID password to sign in to Windows Live Messenger on your Xbox 360 console.

note

Windows Live Messenger uses the Windows Live ID that is attached to your Xbox LIVE account.

4. Select New Conversation, or select an existing conversation as listed on screen.
5. Select the contact with whom you want to begin a chat.
6. To chat with your contact, follow the instructions.

If you are using Windows Live Messenger, you can see the Gamertags of friends logged in to Xbox Live, including the games they are playing.

Windows Live Mail

Windows Live Mail is an email program intended to be the successor for Outlook Express on XP and Windows Mail on Vista. Windows Live Mail has all the features Windows Mail had, plus the following new features:

- Support for other web-based email packages, including Windows Live Hotmail, Gmail (Google Mail), and Yahoo! Mail Plus.

- A user interface that looks like the other Windows Live applications, as shown in Figure 7.2.

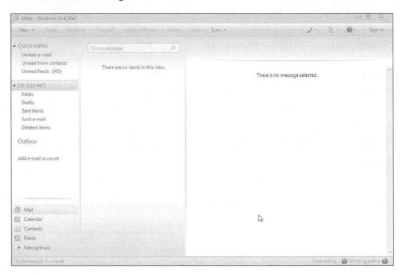

FIGURE 7.2

Windows Live Mail lets you send and receive email the way you did under other email providers, but with new features.

- Synchronization with Windows Live Contacts.

- Support for RSS feeds. This includes the capability to reply directly via email to the author of an item that appears in an RSS feed and the capability to aggregate multiple feeds into a single folder. The RSS functionality requires at least Internet Explorer 7.

- Multiline message lists, the way they worked in Outlook.

- The capability to include emoticons (such as smileys or winks) in emails and other functions.

- Spell checking while creating messages.

- Separate inbox folders for different POP accounts.

- Better support for sending picture files in emails, including basic photo correction and application of different border effects to pictures.

Windows Live Mail also features a new calendaring function. Calendar events are automatically synchronized between Windows Live Mail and Windows Live Calendar.

Windows Live Photo Gallery

Windows Live Photo Gallery is a photo management and sharing application. It is an upgraded version of the Photo Gallery that was part of Vista (see Figure 7.3).

FIGURE 7.3

Windows Live Photo Gallery helps you manage and share your photos.

Windows Live Photo Gallery lets you manage, tag, and search for digital photos. It provides an image viewer that can replace the default Windows 7 image viewer and a tool that lets you download photos from a camera or other removable media.

Windows Live Photo Gallery lets you share photos by uploading them to Windows Live Photos and Flickr. It also lets you upload your pictures to other photo sharing sites such as Facebook via some add-in software. You must have Windows Live Photo Gallery to download full-resolution photos and albums from Windows Live Spaces. You also can publish videos to Soapbox on MSN Video.

New features in Windows Live Photo Gallery include the following:

- A photo/video import tool that enables you to view, select, and tag photos that are automatically grouped by date taken
- The capability to adjust the shadows, highlights, and sharpness in a photo

- The capability to stitch together photos for a panoramic view
- The ability to resize photos and rotate videos
- Support for displaying QuickTime videos when QuickTime 7 is installed
- Face detection, which helps you search your hard drive (or drives) for images containing a particular person

Windows Live Photo Gallery also integrates with Windows Live Sync and enables you to synchronize your photo library with two or more computers that have Photo Gallery installed and signed in on the same Windows Live ID.

Windows Live Writer

Windows Live Writer is a desktop blog publishing application (see Figure 7.4). Its features include WYSIWYG authoring, photo publishing, and map publishing.

Live Writer contains a full set of tools for blogging. If you can use Microsoft Word, you can use Live Writer. An easy-to-use interface lets you format blog entries without having to learn how to use a bunch of new features. With Live Writer, you can

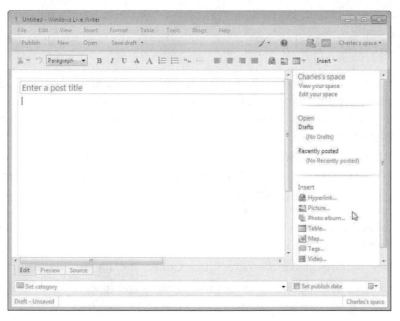

FIGURE 7.4

Live Writer lets you easily create and post to a blog.

- Upload pictures or videos easily from your PC to Soapbox on MSN Video or YouTube. You can load them into your blog quickly without ever opening a browser or leaving Live Writer.

- Automate your blog posting so that new posts are added even if you aren't around to do so. With Live Writer, you can schedule blogs to post on a future date so you can plan for new entries even if you won't be online. You can compose your blog entries while you're commuting, for instance, and publish them when you're back online.

- See your blog theme while you compose and edit, so you can see how your blog post will look before you publish it. Any photos, video links, maps, tags, and other rich media you insert are automatically published when you post.

- Use multiple ways to manipulate text and graphics. For example, if you want to insert something, you can use the Insert tab in the top taskbar, the Insert item on the Compose taskbar, or the Insert item on the Sidebar menu.

- Use the Format tab in the taskbar at the top of the screen to set up fonts, numbering, bullets, and block quotes. You can also do this from the Compose Screen taskbar.

Windows Live Toolbar

The Windows Live Toolbar makes your browsing experience a lot easier by organizing your open websites under grouped tabs, mapping all of the addresses on the web page you're viewing, giving you instant feeds about topics you care about, letting you use more existing buttons and create new ones so you can get the information you care about, and protecting you against phishing and viruses.

It is the successor to the MSN Search Toolbar and indexes all files and emails and runs in the background. The simple search interface starts to list its results as you type in a search query, making it easy to search across emails, pictures, text files, and documents with a single search phrase (see Figure 7.5).

FIGURE 7.5

The Live Toolbar gives you access to all of the Windows Live features.

Unlike many other applications, the Windows Live Toolbar can also be installed on most browsers, letting you quickly link to any of the Windows Live applications from outside.

Windows Live Family Safety

Windows Live Family Safety includes features such as website blocking, content filtering, and web activity monitoring reports found in a number of parental supervision packages (see Figure 7.6). In addition, it provides expert guidance from respected child-oriented organizations (such as the American Academy of Pediatrics) on age-appropriate settings and online activities.

FIGURE 7.6

Keep your children safe with the website filtering, content filtering, and web activity monitoring tools included with Windows Live Family Safety.

Family Safety also provides contact management, where parents are able to create "allow" lists to help prevent their children from communicating with unknown contacts and instead communicate only with contacts that parents have approved. Family Safety allows remote access to its features from anywhere in the world.

From the Family Safety window, allowable members can access the other Windows Live features, as well as use the file sharing abilities of SkyDrive (see the section "SkyDrive").

Windows Live Movie Maker

Live Movie Maker

Windows Live Movie Maker is software that lets you create and edit videos. It replaces the Vista Windows Movie Maker and is not compatible with versions of Windows prior to Vista. However, when its beta version was released in January 2009, user reactions were negative enough that Microsoft decided not to release further versions until the full release of Windows 7.

Windows Live Movie Maker lets you create effects, transitions, titles/ credits, audio track, and timeline narration (see Figure 7.7). You can create new effects, make transitions, and modify existing ones. It also has a basic audio track editing program and can apply basic effects, such as fade in or fade out, to audio tracks. You can export the audio tracks in the form of a sound file instead of a video file.

FIGURE 7.7

Windows Live Movie Maker allows you to create your own movie clips.

To start, you pick either a storyboard view or a timeline view. When in storyboard view, the video project appears as a film strip showing each scene in clips

The strip consists of one video (with accompanying audio bar), one music/audio bar, and one titles/credits bar. In each bar, you can add clips for editing (for example, a .wav music file will belong on the music/audio bar). You can import still images into the timeline and multiply it into any desired number of frames. You can cut the video and music/audio bars into any number of short segments, which will play together seam-lessly when assembled. However the individual segments are actually iso-lated so that, for example, you can lower the music volume briefly while someone is speaking.

When importing footage into the program, you can either choose to capture video (from a camera, a scanner, or some other device) or import into collections to copy existing video files into your collections.

> **tip**
>
> One limitation of Live Movie Maker is that the importing and editing process depends on the amount of file fragmentation on your hard disk: the more fragmented your hard disk, the slower the process. If you plan to do a lot of importing and editing, plan to add an extra hard disk dedicated to scratch storage, and regularly reformat/defragment it.

After capturing a clip, you can drag and drop it anywhere on the timeline. After they are on the timeline, you can duplicate or split clips, and you can use the standard Windows keyboard shortcuts to delete, copy, or drag any of the split sections to another position. Right-clicking any clip brings up the range of editing options.

Windows Live Sync

Windows Live Sync (formerly known as Windows Live FolderShare) is a free file synchronization program that allows files and folders on two or more computers to be in sync with each other.

A maximum of 20 folders (or "libraries") may be synced, including libraries shared over the Internet. Each library can contain a maximum of 20,000 files, and each file cannot exceed 4GB.

New features of Windows Live Sync include the following:

- The capability to sync up to 20 folders with 20,000 files each
- Integration with Windows Live ID
- Integration with the Recycle Bin
- New client versions for both Windows and Mac
- Unicode support
- Integration with Windows Live Photo Gallery to sync photo albums between PCs

SkyDrive

In previous versions of Windows Live Messenger, you could share files with another user via the sharing folder window. When files were added to the sharing folder for that particular person, the file automatically was transferred to the corresponding computer when the other computer was online. This meant that the folder was available to both computers. If a user deleted a shared file, for example, that file was also deleted from the corresponding computer's sharing folder.

The Sharing Folder feature has been discontinued in the latest version of Windows Live Messenger (2009) and is replaced with access to Windows Live SkyDrive instead (see Figure 7.8). SkyDrive is a separate download-able application that lets you use a shareable 25GB space elsewhere (an example of "cloud computing") for files and folders, including photos, that you want to share with others.

FIGURE 7.8

Share up to 25GB of data with anyone you like via SkyDrive.

Password-protected and bundled with an antivirus program, SkyDrive keeps track of other users you've identified as people with whom you're willing to share files, and it lets you know of any new additions, deletions, or changes to the material in your shared folders. You can choose people from your lists in a number of social networks, including Facebook, MySpace, LinkedIn, Hi5, and Tagged, among others.

SkyDrive provides the following features:

- 25GB of storage
- Individual file sizes up to 50MB
- Folders
- Permissions at folder levels
- Permissions at file levels
- Shared folders
- Public folders
- Access permissions within social networks

- Addition of photos directly from Windows Live Photo Gallery
- Prints that can be ordered directly from SkyDrive through HP Snapfish

Office Outlook Connector 12.1

Microsoft Office Outlook Connector is a free add-in for Microsoft Outlook that lets users access Windows Live Hotmail or Office Live Mail accounts through Microsoft Outlook.

With Outlook Connector, you can access email messages and contacts in any Hotmail account for free.

Office Live Add-In

The Office Live Add-in consists of two services, Office Live Workspace and Office Live Small Business. It is available for Windows 7 and Windows Vista, but not for Windows XP.

Office Live Workspace

With Office Live Workspace, you can manage documents from remote locations without schlepping a USB drive from computer to computer (see Figure 7.9). After you install Office Live Update, you can directly access workspaces from Office Word, Excel, and PowerPoint. Files can't be edited from within the workspace, but clicking Edit opens them up in the relevant package. To prevent simultaneous overwriting, documents are checked out and checked in.

FIGURE 7.9

Office Live Workspace allows you to edit documents from anywhere and share those documents with other people you choose.

With Office Live Workspace, you can save up to 5GB of information. This can save you from using USB drives or CDs as a storage solution and lets you update project schedules, organize events, and delegate assignments without scheduling a meeting or relying on email.

Office Live Workspace users can share multiple documents and collaborate online as a group. Workspaces are password-protected, and users can control who views and edits information. Files or workspaces can be shared with up to 100 people.

Office Live Workspace also allows users to store documents of file types other than those generated by Word, Excel, PowerPoint, or Outlook. After the Office Live update is installed, you can open files from Microsoft Office XP, 2003, or 2007 and store them directly. You can also synchronize contacts, tasks, and event lists with Outlook 2003 and 2007 and export workspace lists to Excel.

Office Live Small Business

Microsoft Office Live Small Business is an Internet-based service designed so that nontechnical web users can create a professional-looking website (see Figure 7.10), manage contacts with customers, and utilize a storage area for documents and other files to make them easy for collaboration.

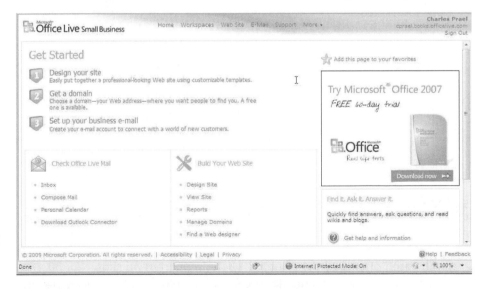

FIGURE 7.10

Even if you're not a highly technical user, Office Live Small Business will help you create a professional website.

Live Small Business provides access to free online web design tools and templates for website development. Site Designer lets you use page layouts, colors, navigation, and other site elements. You can also add modules such as PayPal buttons, blogs, and calendars to pages. Microsoft provides free website hosting and 5GB of storage space for site files, and you can buy more storage space if needed. However, as of 2010, Microsoft will charge an annual fee for website development registration.

With Office Live Small Business, you can select and register domain names and business email addresses. If you already have a domain name with another provider, you can redirect it to Office Live Small Business. Up to 100 domain-based email accounts are allowed at no charge.

The Contact Manager organizes customer information, contact histories, and sales information in one place, with data accessible by permission to entire organizations.

The Team Workspace creates a password-protected project website for posting information to share with customers, employees, or business partners (see Figure 7.11). It helps streamline the editing process and gives remote users access to company data.

FIGURE 7.11
Use the Team Workspace to post information to share with customers, employees, or business partners.

Microsoft offers 24-hour technical phone support at no charge for 30 days. Online, the Community site includes a blog, a wiki, articles, how-to videos, and a customer question and answer space. Office Live Small Business user data is stored on the Microsoft network and is automatically backed up daily.

Silverlight

Microsoft Silverlight is a programmable web browser plug-in that allows you to add multimedia, animation, vector graphics, interactivity, and audio/video playback to your web pages. Designed primarily for those who program interactive and/or animated graphics for web pages, it is a programming environment. Windows 7 comes with an opening slide-show that was done in Silverlight and demonstrates some of the features of this application.

Silverlight lets you play back WMV, WMA, and MP3 content on supported Windows and Mac OSx browsers without requiring Windows Media Player, the Windows Media Player ActiveX control, or the Windows Media browser plug-ins. In Silverlight applications, user interfaces are declared in XAML and programmed using a subset of the .NET Framework. You can use XAML for creating vector graphics and animation. Text created with Silverlight is searchable and indexable by search engines.

Windows Media Center

Windows Media Center lets you turn your PC into an all-in-one center for control of your entertainment devices. This means that you can use your PC to access music, photos, TV, movies, and other online media from the comfort of your couch with your remote control. It also lets you stream music, TV, movies, photos, and other entertainment to such devices as your cell phone, as well as email, text, and messages.

Windows Media Center is the environment in which you play digital media, as well as organize the media files, burn CD-ROMs, and synchronize your files with multiple devices.

Windows Media Player

By far the most often used part of Windows Media Center is the Windows Media Player (see Figure 7.12).

Starting with Vista, Microsoft included a digital media player that lets you download, edit, rearrange, and watch photos, videos, or movies or listen to recorded music and commercial radio. Some users no longer subscribe to cable or satellite TV and now watch TV via their computers.

With a simple USB TV Tuner, you can record and watch shows on your schedule. Windows Media Center has been updated to manage a single TV guide containing both standard and digital high-definition TV shows.

FIGURE 7.12

Windows Media Player shows your entire media library in one consolidated interface.

You start the Media Player by clicking the related icon in the taskbar. The first time you do this, you'll be asked to set up the Windows Media Player, which may take some time. After it is set up, you can click this icon to display a list of frequently accessed sections of Media Center. This can be either specific files, such as photos and videos, or functions, such as TV.

You can toggle back and forth between full-screen and minimized modes by clicking anywhere on the content that is playing. Or you can click the View Full Screen icon on the right side of the media controls.

To view your full Media Library along with the interface for managing it, click the Switch To Library icon on the right side of the media controls. After you switch to the Library View, you get the full screen for managing your library.

In Figure 7.12, the primary categories in the digital media library are on the left, what's currently playing is minimized on the right, and the controls for what's playing are in the bar at the bottom.

After you pick a category, you'll be able to find your favorite shows quickly with new features such as turbo scroll. Just hold down the right-arrow key and you'll zip through content listings.

---

note

Windows 7 now supports many types of media files, including .asf, .wma, .wmv, .wm, metafiles (.asx, .wax, .wvx, .wpl), Microsoft Digital Video Recording (.dvr-ms), .wmd, .avi, and MPG-type files (.mpg, .mpeg, .m1v, .mp2, .mp3, .mpa, .mpe, .mpv2, and .m3u). In addition, it supports .aac audio files and H.264, DivX, and Xvid video files, with no third-party download needed.

Play To

You can use the Windows 7 Media Player to send video or audio to other Windows 7 PCs and DLNA (Digital Living Network Alliance)-certified digital media rendering devices via the Play To feature (see Figure 7.13). With Play To, you can browse or search from within Windows Media Player or Windows Explorer to find the media you want and then choose where you want it to be played. A remote control window appears for each Play To session, giving you the ability to control the entire experience.

FIGURE 7.13

Use the Play To feature to send video or audio to other devices.

You can also Play To a cell phone, provided it is DLNA-certified and supports Windows 7. After you've set up the Windows Media Player to stream media to the cell phone, you can select media items to play on a cell phone or another PC. A Play To remote control window appears on the cell phone, providing standard controls like play, pause, stop, skip forward and backward, seek forward and backward, volume, and mute. After the Play To remote control window appears on your cell phone, you can reorder or delete items, add to the queue, or toggle repeat. You can even add new media items from Windows Media Player or Windows Explorer by dragging them into this window.

Streaming Media

Streaming media is pictures, audio, video, or other media that is constantly received by a user while it is being delivered by a streaming provider. Microsoft has been providing support for streaming media since the 1980s, although there have been problems with bandwidth and computers powerful enough to handle that much data that fast. Windows XP and Vista provided some support for streaming media; Windows 7 provides much better support.

In Windows 7, media streaming is enabled and works by default. Configuring media streaming is easy. The Stream menu in the Window Media Player user interface (see Figure 7.14) enables you to

- Set up your home PC so you can access your media libraries while away from home.

- Allow other Windows 7 PCs and devices to push media to your Player and control it.

- Quickly authorize all home PCs and devices to access your media collection.

FIGURE 7.14
Allow Windows Media Player to be controlled from another location.

After you have the Windows Media Player configured to allow streaming media anywhere in your house (or office), why stop there? If your pictures, music, videos, and recorded TV content are available on your home PC, you take it with you, say, on a family vacation. You don't have to download what you want onto your laptop or other media player. You can tap into the entertainment on your home PC from pretty much wherever you can connect to the Internet. Use Windows Media Player on your laptop to listen to music and view pictures, videos, or recorded TV in the media libraries on your home PC.

Internet Explorer 8

In a concerted effort to match and beat the features of other browsers (notably Firefox), Internet Explorer 8 has added some unique, convenient new ways to access web resources with Accelerators and Web Slices. It has a color-coded tab system, an improved address bar, and enhanced privacy protections, in addition to some new security and web helper features (see Figure 7.15).

FIGURE 7.15

Internet Explorer 8 includes a variety of new features similar to other popular browsers, such as Firefox.

> **note**
>
> Internet Explorer 8 features, such as Accelerators and Web Slices, are covered in more detail in Chapter 6.

Accelerators

Accelerators are basically in-page web services—a way to get relevant information without having to leave your current page. Highlight some text and a blue arrow icon pops up nearby. Click this and you'll see a list of actions, such as search, map, or blog. Choose an action, such as map, and the map pops up when you highlight its entry in the list of actions.

Web Slices

Web Slices enable you to see frequently updated web data, such as eBay listings or sections of a news site. When your mouse moves over a content area on a page that supports this IE8 feature, a green box appears around content that has been programmed to allow Web Slices. Clicking the nearby green button enables you to create a Web Slice for the content, using the toolbar to drop down updated information about the item at any time.

The slice also appears in your Feed sidebar, which you can access from the star at the top left of the browser.

Colored Tabs

When you have several tabs open and launch a new one from within one of the open tabs, the color of the just-created tab will match that of its parent. All like-colored tabs are grouped together, so your new tab may not appear all the way to the right the way you're used to. After you've gotten used to the change, it's a helpful visual cue not found in competing products. When you close the tab of the page you're viewing, the new focus will be a related tab, not just the one to the right or left.

When you create a tab, you can initiate a variety of useful actions that include reopening closed tabs, starting InPrivate browsing (which doesn't save the session to your History), or choosing an Accelerator. And IE8 is still the only major browser that lets you choose to close just the current tab rather than all of them when you hit the X close icon.

A new find-on-page capability lets you jump to each subsequent occurrence of your search text. This feature also lets you choose whether to match case or only whole words entered.

InPrivate Browsing

InPrivate Browsing hides activity from your browser history when enabled. You can turn on InPrivate Browsing when you open a blank tab or from the Safety menu, and a bar next to the address bar clearly shows you've enabled this browsing mode.

InPrivate Filtering

InPrivate Filtering prevents third-party websites, which may supply content to the page you're visiting, from gathering information from your browsing session. You can even choose the sites you'll allow to access such data. You can enable or disable InPrivate Filtering without turning on InPrivate Browsing, via an icon at the bottom of the program's window.

When you clear private data, you can erase most of it while still keeping your login and settings information for sites in your Favorites.

The SmartScreen filter blocks both phishing and malware-distributing sites. When you land on either, you see a red page with a warning, rather than being taken to the site. If you're unsure about a site, you can check it from the Safety menu, where you can also report destinations that you've determined contain malware.

With cross-site scripting (XSS), you might get an email, for example, with a link to a legitimate site, such as that of a store. However, characters appended to the URL run a script that could send your keystrokes to the malware writer or other destinations. When such an attack is detected, IE8 automatically refuses to execute the related script code and alerts you that an attack has been blocked.

note

Clickjacking is a form of tricking an Internet user into revealing confidential information or taking control of the computer. This happens when you click what appears to be a normal button but is actually an overlay in a frame covering the button. You might bump into this in one of your online accounts, such as an online store. IE8 lets website owners prevent third-party sites from placing such frames, while still giving you an option to view the site in a separate window.

8

Windows 7 Security

Security has become a bigger and bigger issue because of the prolif-
eration of methods for finding out private information that's stored
on your computer. Practices that used to be reserved for highly specialized IT professionals are now virtually required on every home
and small business computer.

This chapter discusses security issues in both Windows 7 and Internet
Explorer 8. It also discusses some security features that were introduced in Windows Vista but have been improved in Windows 7.

> **note**
>
> Remember that this book is aimed at the home and small business user,
> not at IT professionals. The coverage here is meant to provide a jumping
> off point for the typical consumer and not intended to be inclusive of all
> Windows 7's security features. If you want to take a deeper dive into
> Windows security, we suggest that you pick up a copy of *Microsoft*
> *Windows 7 Unleashed*, published by Sams, or *Microsoft Windows 7 In*
> *Depth*, published by Que.

New Security Features in Windows 7

Microsoft has included a bevy of new security features and enhance-
ments. If you are coming to Windows 7 from Windows Vista, the
changes won't seem as daunting as to those coming to 7 from XP.
However, previous Vista users will appreciate the toned down User
Account Control (UAC) system that was much maligned by
Windows users and scoffed at by Mac users.

Whereas previous security provisions were located in several Windows application areas, in Windows 7 all the security features are integrated into the Action Center, a central place to look for various kinds of security settings. You can see the Action Center by choosing Start, System and Security, Action Center.

The Action Center

The Action Center is the first icon on the left on the Control Panel and includes alerts and configuration settings for the Security Center, Windows Defender, Network Access Protection, and User Account Control. It continually monitors these security settings and displays a pop-up balloon if it detects a problem.

Windows Defender: Checking for Spyware and Viruses

When you open the Action Center window, the first thing you see on the right is a set of messages indicating problems you should resolve (see Figure 8.1). Frequently this will involve updating protection from spyware and unwanted software or updating your virus protection. Where it's important that you resolve the problem, a red bar appears next to the message, and you'll see various suggested options.

Clicking the Update Now button in one of the boxes with a red bar launches an antispyware program that scans your computer for malicious software and deletes or quarantines any malware it finds.

Windows Defender comes with options that let you automatically update the security scan and schedule regular system scans to protect your computer system. You can define default actions for low, medium, and high alerts that will be automatically executed by the program. There are also links to the Windows Defender website, where you can get more security tools and the latest security information, and to the Microsoft Malware Protection Center, for updated information on malware.

Click the left-arrow to return to the Action Center to see more security options.

Change Action Settings

On the Action Center, the first option, Change Action Settings, lets you determine which kinds of problems you want monitored (see Figure 8.2). For each item you check, Windows periodically looks for problems and displays a message if problems are found.

Actions needing immediate attention
are marked with red bars

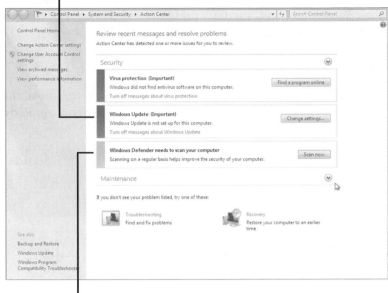

Actions needing attention soon
are marked with yellow bars

FIGURE 8.1

The Action Center groups a variety of Windows security features under one umbrella.

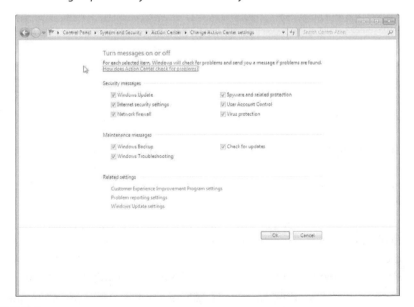

FIGURE 8.2

You can tell Windows which kinds of alerts you want to receive.

Although it's a good idea to check everything at first, eventually you'll get tired of seeing repeated warning messages, especially when the messages are about situations that don't present a real danger. This is the window where you can turn these messages on and off, by category.

Change User Account Control Settings

This window is useful when some of your programs can make changes to your computer, either because you allow it or when some program automatically updates itself.

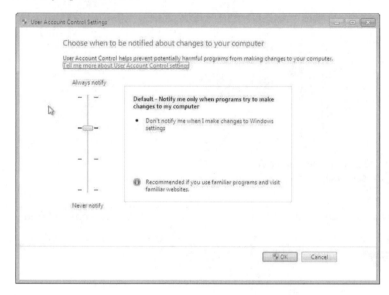

FIGURE 8.3

Use this slider to adjust the kinds of notices you get when one or more of your programs is replaced or changed.

The bar on the left is a sliding scale, indicating how much control you want to have over these notifications. As you move the slider, you'll see messages indicating what that level of control corresponds to, in terms of warnings.

Normally we don't suggest that people read the Tell me more... links the first time they use a program. Here we suggest that you do click on Tell me more about User Account Control settings because information will show you how to use the slider on the User Account Control screen.

For instance, if you set the slider to Always notify, you'll probably quickly get tired of all the notices, the fact that your screen dims each time there's a notice, and the fact that you have to approve or deny each request before you can do anything else. On the other hand, "Never notify" means that:

- If you're logged on as the administrator, any program can make changes without your knowing about it, or

- If you're logged on as a user, any changes that require an administrator's permission will be denied.

View Archived Messages

If you have archived messages about problems that have been reported to Microsoft, you'll see them here. The messages are stored by date. If you want to keep other kinds of messages in the archive, use the Change Action Center Settings window.

View Performance Information

The Performance Indicators are the result of a measurement of your computer's hardware and software configuration. The overall measurement is called a Base Score and can range from 1.0 to 10, depending on what you have installed. A higher base score means that your computer will perform better and faster than one with a lower base score, especially when doing something requiring a lot of resources.

Each hardware component also receives a score, and the lowest such score determines the base score. (For example, if you don't have a gaming graphics board, you'll get a 1.0 score for that piece of hardware and your base score will therefore be 1.0.)

Various options below the numbers let you interpret the numbers, find tips for improving your system's performance, or view and print detailed information about your system's performance. In addition, you can change the visual effects, adjust the indexing options, adjust your power settings, clean up your hard disk(s), and use other tools.

BitLocker To Go

BitLocker is another security feature originally introduced with Windows Vista that protects against data theft or exposure on computers that are lost or stolen, and it offers more secure data deletion when computers are decommissioned.

New with Windows 7 is BitLocker To Go, which applies the same protection to portable storage devices, such as the ubiquitous thumb drive. Files on devices protected by BitLocker To Go cannot be modified unless the user enters the appropriate password (or uses the appropriate smart card).

You can set up BitLocker with the BitLocker Drive Encryption option on the left side of the Control Panel.

Encrypting your files has both positive and negative implications. On the plus side, it can mean hackers can't get at the system files they need to discover and change your passwords or move your files to a device they can access. On the minus side, it also means that you have to remember your passwords in order to simply use your files. And writing down passwords makes it easier for someone else to discover your passwords.

BitLocker can protect entire drives, such as the drive on which you installed Windows. It can be used to protect internal hard drives, too. However, BitLocker To Go lets you also encrypt removable drives, such as USB drives. As long as you use the password you set up, you have access to files stored on such a drive while others don't have access. If you add files to an encrypted drive, those files will fall under the encryption protection, too.

Direct Access

If you use your computer at home or on the road and access a corporate network from time to time, DirectAccess automatically establishes a connection between your computer and the corporate network. When connected with DirectAccess, you have a seamless, secure path to the corporate network whenever you are connected to the Internet, without creating a virtual private network (VPN).

If you need tools or data that's normally stored on a corporate network, for instance, but today you're working in the coffee shop located at the beach, you can have your data and your beach backdrop, too. Based on security credentials you establish when you install Direct Access, you can seamlessly get through corporate firewalls in order to access the information you need.

Further, if you connect to a corporate network that automatically updates your laptop with company-verified software, links to company files, and security programs, Direct Access makes this transparent, even if you're not logged on—each time you connect to the Internet, the updates are loaded onto your computer automatically.

Finally, Direct Access helps corporate security officers ensure that the computers of remote users still meet the security and system health requirements of a corporate environment.

Credentials Manager

The Credentials Manager, on the Control Panel, stores your user IDs and passwords safely in the Windows Vault, where they can't be retrieved by keystroke capture programs or other spyware. Older versions of Windows allowed you to set cookies or other automated procedures that let you quickly log in to password-protected websites and use private documents and other files, but the cookies files could be accessed by spyware and other programs.

With Windows Vault storing these IDs and passwords, any Windows application that needs credentials to access a resource (for example, a server or a website) can use the Credentials Manager instead of prompting you to enter your ID and password each time or retrieve that information from an accessible cookie file.

Windows Vault stores credentials that Windows can log in the users automatically, which means that any Windows application that needs credentials to access a resource (server or a website) can make use of this Credential Manager & Windows Vault and use the credentials supplied instead of a user having to enter a username and password each time. However, this applies only to Windows applications, not to external programs such as Facebook, Twitter, Gmail, and so on, that can automatically log in a user via cookies set by a browser.

You can also back up and restore the Vault, such as to a USB thumb drive, so that your security can be regenerated if your system crashes.

Windows Live Family Safety

We discussed Windows Live Family Safety previously, in Chapter 7, "New Windows 7 Applications." Briefly, with Windows Live Family Safety you can block websites, filter content, and monitor web activity for anyone using your computer. Additionally, you can create lists of people with whom other users are allowed contact, effectively letting you approve anyone they want to chat or exchange email with.

SkyDrive

SkyDrive keeps track of other users you've identified as people with whom you're willing to share files, and it lets you know of any new additions, deletions, or changes to the material in your shared folders. SkyDrive comes password-protected and bundled with an antivirus program. You can choose people from your lists in a number of social networks, including Facebook, MySpace, LinkedIn, Hi5, and Tagged, among others.

SkyDrive is covered in more detail in Chapter 7.

Fingerprint Scanning

A growing number of computers, particularly portable computers, include embedded fingerprint readers. Fingerprint readers can be used for identification and authentication.

Windows Vista allowed fingerprint scanners to be implemented, thus enabling only specific people to use a computer. Windows 7 makes it easier for end users to set up, configure, and manage fingerprint scanners. Consult the documentation that came with your scanner for details.

Smart Cards

A smart card is something like an ATM debit card, in that it holds information about you and what you're allowed to do. In terms of business and home computers, it lets you protect sensitive data so that only those with the permissions granted by the smart card can have access to that data. At home, for instance, you may allow your children to use your computer for certain things, but only with your smart card could anyone read, modify, and save sensitive financial data.

Windows 7 users can use smart cards from those vendors that have published their drivers through Windows Update without needing special modification software. These drivers can be downloaded in the same way as drivers for other devices in Windows.

Unlike Windows Vista, Windows 7 automatically installs the drivers required to support smart cards and smart card readers it detects without invoking any administrative permissions. Windows 7 supports the national Plug and Play and Personal Identity Verification (PIV) standards. When a PIV-compliant smart card is inserted into a smart card reader, Windows attempts to download the driver from Windows Update. If an appropriate driver is not available from Windows Update, a PIV-compliant minidriver that is included with Windows 7 is used for the card.

In the Windows 7 Enterprise and Windows 7 Ultimate operating systems, you can choose to encrypt your removable media by turning on BitLocker and then choosing the Smart Card option to unlock the drive. At runtime, Windows retrieves the correct minidriver for the smart card and allows the operation to complete.

New Security Features in Internet Explorer 8

Internet Explorer 8 now includes new anti-malware protection and better ways to protect your privacy.

InPrivate Browsing

When enabled, InPrivate Browsing hides activity from your browser history. When you turn on InPrivate Browsing, a bar next to the address bar shows you've enabled this browsing mode (see Figure 8.4). This means that your browser history will not retain the addresses of sites you've visited.

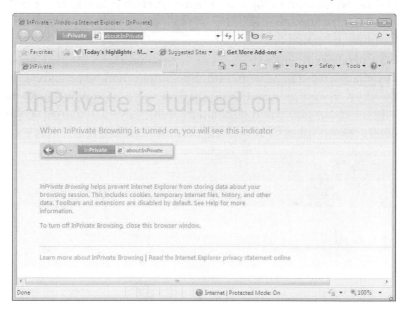

FIGURE 8.4

When InPrivate Browsing is enabled, you'll see this notifier in the address bar.

Some websites gather information about you when you visit the site. InPrivate Filtering prevents these sites, which may supply content to the page you're visiting, from doing so. You can also choose the sites you'll allow to collect your data. You can enable or disable InPrivate Filtering without turning on InPrivate Browsing by clicking the icon at the bottom of the program's window.

SmartScreen

The SmartScreen filter blocks both phishing and malware-distributing sites. Phishing involves sending an email to a user and falsely claiming to be an established legitimate enterprise in an attempt to trick the user into surrendering private information that will be used for identity theft. The email directs you to visit a website where you are asked to update personal information, such as passwords and credit card numbers, your

Social Security number, or bank account numbers. This website is bogus and steals your information, usually transferring it to identity thieves.

Malware sites contain rogue programs that can plant Trojan horses, viruses, or other destructive applications in your computer. These programs pose a major security threat to Internet security internationally and are proliferating yearly. Your best protection is to stay away from these sites, but because new ones are created all the time, your problem is identifying the new ones.

With Windows 7, when you land on either a phishing site or a malware site, you see a red page with a warning, rather than being taken to the site. If you're unsure about a site, you can check it from the Safety menu, where you can also report destinations that you've determined contain malware (see Figure 8.5).

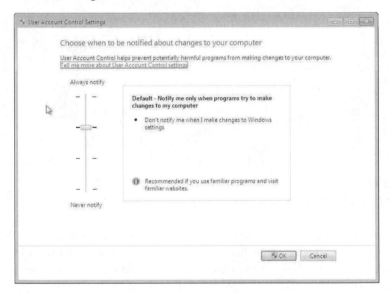

FIGURE 8.5

SmartScreen Filter will check sites that you aren't sure about and will flag you if you attempt to visit a known dangerous site.

With cross-site scripting (XSS), you might get an email, for example, with a link to a legitimate site, such as that of a store. However, characters appended to the URL run a script that could send your keystrokes to the malware writer or other destinations. When such an attack is detected, IE8 automatically refuses to execute the related script code and alerts you that an attack has been blocked.

Microsoft Security Essentials

With Windows 7, Microsoft has released a new, free, antivirus suite, Microsoft Security Essentials (MSE). MSE is an outgrowth of Windows Live Onecare, which was recently discontinued. MSE is designed to provide protection against viruses, spyware, rootkits, and Trojan horse attacks. One Care was a suite of applications that included a firewall, backup, tune up, multi-PC management, simplified Wi-Fi security configuration, and simplified printer sharing. Most of the functions supplied by One Care were reassigned under Windows 7 to other portions of the system software.

After it is installed, MSE provides protection for both of the primary avenues of infection:

- Real-time scanning protects against email and web-based delivery of viruses and other causes of infection.

- System scanning protects your system against any already resident viruses, as well as any attacks that are delivered by other means, such as infected thumb drives.

One security issue is that system scanning of removable drives is not enabled by default. You should enable this option immediately after you install MSE.

Before downloading and installing MSE, you will need to make sure that your system has passed Microsoft's Windows Genuine Advantage antipiracy scanner, and you must register for a free Windows Live account.

note

To learn more about Microsoft Security Essentials, be sure to check out the e-book, Microsoft Security Essentials User Manual, by Michael Miller, available at www.informit.com.

A Word about File Sharing

In these days of collaboration, it's common to need an environment where you can share files with one or more other users. However, whenever you open your computer to access by another person or another computer, you have the potential for a breach of security.

There are a lot of simple ways to share files, such as emailing a copy of a file to another person, or putting the file on removable media, or even using a dedicated space for file sharing. There are always problems with these approaches:

- What happens when two or more users make changes to a file at the same time and neither knows about the other's changes? Merging both sets of changes into a single, common file is never fun and can occasionally wind up with dueling changes going back and forth.

- If you both use a common password, how can you be sure that the other person doesn't give someone else access to the secure area?

- If you use file-sharing software that leaves your computer open, someone else can potentially put a file on your computer that you don't want there. We've seen examples of this range from the mundane (someone storing their music collection on a shared directory that opened up for a school writing composition class) to the hazardous (viruses using this method to spread themselves to new computers). We've even seen a few cases where this particular problem got someone in trouble with the courts.

- If you also have your computer on a wireless network, we've seen cases of completely unknown people trying to use your spare disk space to store their "extra" software. Most often this is harmless (but very annoying), but we're aware of a couple cases where someone wound up hosting several gigabytes of someone else's porn collection because they had inadvertently failed to secure their file sharing.

As you might guess from the above, we're strong proponents of securing your shared file spaces, when you have them. There are a number of tools available that can also help deal with some of the other issues involved in file sharing—Microsoft Word, for example, has long had a "track changes" option that allows you to track the changes made to a document by different users, allow or deny the changes, and even merge changes from differing documents into a single common document.

9

Windows 7 Networking

Microsoft's developers paid a lot of attention to how PCs are currently used on networks. The result has been more emphasis on making it easier to set up, connect to, and share information on a home network, and by extension connect to other networks and share devices as well. In Chapter 10, "Wireless Networking," we look at wireless networking specifically, but this chapter is more about Windows 7 networking in general.

Setting Up Your Connection

Regardless of what kind of network connection you want to create, your first stop is at the Network and Sharing screen. To get there, follow these steps:

1. Go to the Start Menu and select Control Panel, Network and Internet (see Figure 9.1).

---

note

Note that this is different from the equivalent in Vista, where the process of setting up your network involved selecting specific options, sometimes on the Control Panel and sometimes elsewhere. With Windows 7, the options all start with those listed on the Control Panel. Networking options on the right side of the Control Panel screen list Devices and Printers, HomeGroup, Internet Options, Network and Sharing Center, RemoteApp and Desktop Connections, and Windows Firewall, all of which have something to do with networking.

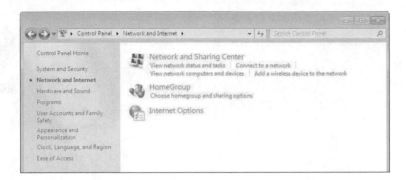

FIGURE 9.1

The Control Panel is your destination when setting up a network under Windows 7.

2.   Click Network and Sharing Center on the right side of the screen (see Figure 9.2). Note that this is different from the Network and Sharing Center that appeared in Vista, as shown in Figure 9.3. In Windows 7, the Network and Sharing Center automatically finds the networks to which your computer is connected. If you're connected to the Internet, you will see the path from your computer via whatever network you're using to the Internet. In the example shown in Figure 9.2, the name of that network was simply "Network." Below that is a list of your currently active networks. If your computer is at home, your home network will appear here, as will any available Wi-Fi connections near your home. Below that is where you set up your network connections, both internal to your home and external to other networks, including the Internet.

3.   In the section labeled View Your Active Networks, click Connect or Disconnect. In the small box on the upper right, the list of networks Windows 7 has detected appears. The ones that are currently active are listed in the top half of the window, and the ones to which you could connect but haven't are in the bottom half. If you want to connect to one of these, this is the place to do it. Simply click the Connect button and enter the information requested. Likewise, if you want to disconnect from one of these networks, do it here and follow the instructions.

Setting Up Your Home Network

Assuming your computer is a laptop that travels with you from home to work, to the local coffee shop or library, or to other locations, one of your first tasks after installing Windows 7 should be setting up your home network.

Windows 7 automatically finds any networks
to which your computer is connected

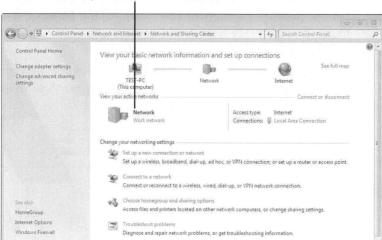

FIGURE 9.2

Windows 7 simplifies network discovery, automatically finding any network to which your computer is connected.

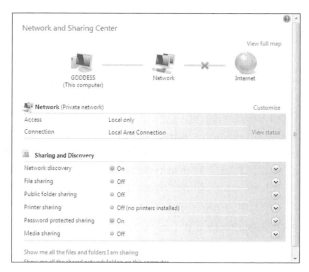

FIGURE 9.3

The Network and Sharing Center in Windows Vista is quite different from what you'll see in Windows 7.

In Windows 7, when you select the Home network profile, your system knows that you are "at home" and will start the essential services required for successful file and printer sharing in the home. This provides an intuitive entry point into HomeGroup, and after you are "at home," the automatic network discovery facility starts looking for other Win7 PCs in the home. If you already have an active HomeGroup, you can join it—or, if not, create one.

When you click Networks and Sharing on the Control Panel and click on the name of the first network (not the icon) shown under View Your Active Networks, you see the screen shown in Figure 9.4.

FIGURE 9.4

The Network and Sharing options let you choose which type of network you want to set up.

Picking one of these types of network does two things:

1. It gives Windows some basic information that allows the system to automatically set up some of the connections and specifications that are normally found in that type of network. You can tailor these specifications later on, but at least you'll have the framework with which you can work.

2. It gives this network a default name (which you can change later).

Basically, your home network is where you're likely to set up two or more computers, a printer, maybe a scanner, maybe some external storage devices, and so on. You can add more connections to other devices, such as an automatic connection to your cell phone or to a wide screen TV, through the Media Center or HomeGroup later on.

Your office network doesn't have to be in a physical office, nor does it have to be in a different place from your home network. This type of network is more about higher levels of security, such as using your laptop in a coffee shop, or connecting to a corporate network to let you work at home.

A public network is also about security. More importantly, it provides additional levels of security to protect your computer from others using the same network, such as might be found in a hotel's network where there are in-room connections.

To set up a home network, follow these steps:

1. If your PC does not have a network adapter (often called a NIC) installed, you will need to install it first. Follow the instructions that came with the adapter. Most likely, however, your computer came with a network adapter already installed.

2. On the Control Panel, click the Network and Sharing option.

3. Select Home Network.

4. If your computer is not already connected to a network, see "Connecting to the Internet for the First Time or Setting Up a New Home Network," later in this chapter.

    If your computer is connected to a network, but you're setting it up so that Windows 7 can recognize it, you'll see a screen like that shown in Figure 9.5 describing the active network, with whatever name (or lack of name) you've given it. (If you have already connected your computer to the network adapter so you can reach the Internet, that connection will be shown here as depicted in Figure 9.5.)

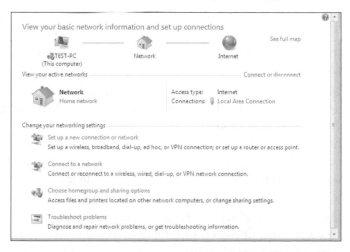

FIGURE 9.5

Set up all your network connections to computers, peripheral devices, and other networks in one place.

note

Note that the top portion of the dialog box shown in Figure 9.5 shows what the system can automatically detect about the network you're setting up. The bottom portion of the screen displays the options you have for your network settings.

The following sections walk you through many of the network setup options available to you. However, understand that networking is an enormous topic and not one that we can cover in its entirety here. If you want to learn more about Windows 7 networking, we suggest you pick up a copy of *Microsoft Windows 7 Unleashed*, by Robert Cowart and Brian Knittel, published by Que.

note

Two other items found on the Network and Sharing screen—Choose HomeGroup and Sharing Options and "Troubleshoot Problems"—are discussed in detail later in this chapter.

Connecting to the Internet for the First Time or Setting Up a New Home Network

Follow these steps if you are connecting to the Internet for the first time or are setting up a new Home Network:

1. Click on Set Up a New Connection or Network. On the next screen choose your connection option.

2. If you're connecting to the Internet for the first time with this computer, select the first option and click the Next button.

3. On the next screen, select Create a New Connection and click the Next button.

4. On the next screen, select the type of connection option you want to use. Since you have already installed your network connector device, you will know what kind of data transmission it is using—broadband, cable modem, Wi-Fi, and so on. Select the appropriate option. If it isn't shown, select Show Connection Options That This Computer Is Not Set Up to Use, and follow the instructions.

5. If you're connecting to the Internet, enter the information from your Internet Service Provider (ISP) and click the Connect button. The system will automatically connect you to the Internet to the default web page with Internet Explorer 8, and you can browse to just about anywhere on the Internet.

6. If you're setting up a new network, be sure you have set up a router or network access device (follow the manufacturer's directions to install it). When it's been set up correctly, navigate to the Home Network screen depicted earlier in Figure 9.4, select Set Up a New Network and click the Next button.

7. On the next screen, Windows 7 lists the wireless routers or other access devices it can detect. Select the one you want to use and click the Next button.

8. Type in any connection information your ISP might have provided you. ISPs will often provide you with a user name and password to secure your login. If they did, then you should enter them at this time. Your connection might not require a login, however, so if your ISP's instructions ignore that issue, you will not need to put that information in here.

Setting Up a Connection to an Existing Network

In order to connect to an existing network, you will need to follow these steps:

1. If this network is to connect to the Internet, set up the connection with a cable or DSL modem and an account with an Internet service provider. You will likely be sharing this connection with other computers in the house, so make sure they are connected to the cable or DSL modem, too. If you're using a cable connection, such as Comcast, you'll receive directions for setting up the hardware and this connection from the service provider. Follow these instructions:

   • If you're using a DSL or other high speed connection, you'll be connecting to a special phone line. If this is provided by your phone company, they will usually provide the connection to the main phone wiring box for your house and you'll need to provide the wiring from there to your computer. You can either string the phone wire yourself (frequently under your house, if you have a basement or crawl space) or have a technician do it. That phone wire will end in a junction box, and your phone company will show you what kind of box this needs to be. You can buy this junction box at most hardware stores.

   • If you'll be using a Wi-Fi connection to the Internet, please see Chapter 10.

   • If you're connecting to an existing network in your house or office, there will be a network connection device to which other computers and devices may be already connected. Simply plug in to the device a cable with an Ethernet connector and plug the other end of the cable into the Ethernet port on your computer.

- Another popular option is to have a wireless connection included as part of your network connection, allowing you to wirelessly connect from anywhere in your home or office.

- Alternately, you may have a more sophisticated network in your home or office, using network switches to connect the computers, printers, and other devices in your home. If so, you will plug your computer into the switch, rather than directly into your network device.

2. Once you've plugged your computer into the network, return to the Network and Sharing screen and choose Connect to a Network.

3. The right side of the screen shows you that you're connected to a network, which might be simply named "Network," unless you've given it a name such as "Home" or "Office." The choices below that indicate the types of network connection you can choose. If you have a DSL or cable connection, Broadband Connection will appear with a blue box around it as shown in Figure 9.6, which means it's the default type of connection. Select it and click the Connect button. If you're connecting to a dial-up modem, or to a VPN network, and you've set up the connection, those choices will appear as blue on this screen. Choose the appropriate one and click the Connect button.

The default connection type is marked with a blue box

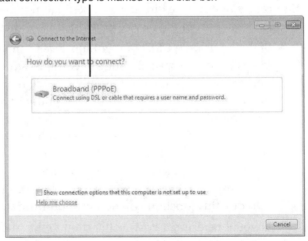

FIGURE 9.6

If you have a broadband connection, it will appear as shown here. Unless you've set up other types of access, this is likely to be the only connection type shown.

4. In either case, the connection will be made and you'll be prompted for a user ID and password. Enter the appropriate information and click the Connect button. Your connection will then be live and you can communicate via the network you just joined.

Connecting to Your Office Network

Follow these steps to connect to your office network:

1. Click on Set Up a New Connection or Network. On the next screen choose your connection option.

2. Select Connect to a Workplace and click the Next button.

3. On the next screen, choose either the Virtual Private Network (VPN) option or the dial-up option. If you already have an Internet connection, the system will use it to set up what amounts to a private tunnel through the Internet to reach your workplace's servers. If you have to dial into the workplace network, you'll need to provide the appropriate phone number that your system can use to place the phone call.

4. If you're using a dial-up connection (usually a modem that automatically dials a phone number to set up a connection), make sure your modem is switched on and connected to a phone line; then select Set Up a Dial-up Connection and click the Next button.

5. Enter the phone number as requested and click the Next button. You will have to provide appropriate login ID and password information each time you connect.

6. In either case, once you've completed the process, you'll have a live connection. You will likely have to provide appropriate login ID and password information each time you connect.

Adding Another Computer to Your Home Network

1. Plug in the connecting cable between the other computer and your network adapter or router. See "Setting Up a Connection to an Existing Network," earlier in this chapter. Windows will automatically try to determine what other computers are on the network and will store that information for you.

2. When the other computer was first started, whoever set up or configured it was required to give it a name (such as Perry, George, Living Room, or something meaningful). That became the system name, and is what your system looks for. Now you need to set up a network connection.

- If you want to connect to another Windows 7 system, you probably want to set up a HomeGroup. See the "Your HomeGroup" later in this chapter for how to set up and connect to a HomeGroup.

- If, however, you want to connect a non-Windows 7 computer, or you don't want to use a HomeGroup, you need to do things a little differently. So start up Windows Explorer by clicking on the Explorer icon on the taskbar as shown in Figure 9.7.

Windows Explorer icon

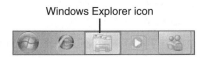

FIGURE 9.7

Start Windows Explorer from the taskbar.

3. Click on the Network item on the left side to see all of the computers (and other network devices) on your local network that your system was able to find as shown in Figure 9.8.

…displays networked computers and devices

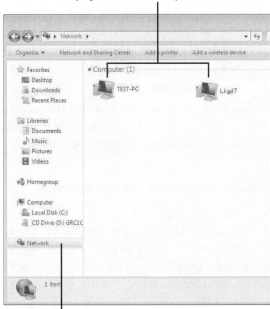

Selecting the network item in the left pane…

FIGURE 9.8

Use Windows Explorer to find systems on your network.

4. Next, click on the system that you want to connect to. You will probably be asked for a user ID and password. What you need to enter is the user name and password from that other system that you want to use to log in.

5. Once you have logged in to the other computer, you can see the various resources that are shared and available on the other computer, as shown in Figure 9.9.

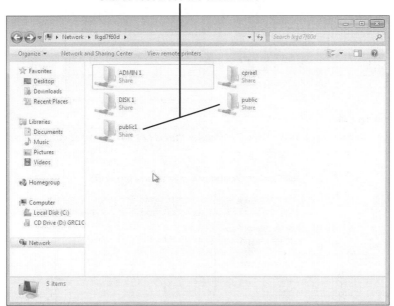

Shared resources are shown here

FIGURE 9.9

Now, you can see shared resources on another networked computer.

Understanding Domains

An additional concept that occasionally can cause problems is that of domains. Domains are used by Windows as a central repository of login information. Within a domain, you can use the same user name and password on all systems in the domain. Windows 7 turns on domains by default—and if you do not connect to an outside domain—declares your Windows 7 system as the controller of the domain.

If you attempt to log in to a non-Windows 7 computer that isn't part of that domain, you will receive a login failure (see Figure 9.10). To work around this problem, you will need to click Use Another Account, and then force the login to be domainless by adding a backslash (\) character in front of the user name (see Figure 9.11).

FIGURE 9.10

Attempting to access a non-Windows 7 computer that is not part of the domain will result in an error.

Add a backslash before the user name and press OK

FIGURE 9.11

You can force a domainless login by choosing Use Another Account and adding a backslash to the username.

Connecting a Printer or Other Device

It's easy to connect a printer either directly to your computer or to the network to which your computer is connected, and to specify how it is to be shared:

1. Connect the printer to your computer or to the network adapter you'll be using. Directions for this are usually on a small pamphlet that comes with your printer.

2. Make sure the appropriate driver for your printer is installed on your computer. (A driver is a piece of software that interprets the data coming from a computer to the printer. Each type of printer needs its own driver.) Install the printer driver by choosing the manufacturer and model of the printer you'll be using. If you don't see it, click the Windows Update button.

   - If you already have the CD containing the printer driver for this printer, insert the disc in the CD or DVD drive and click the Have Disk button. You'll be walked through the steps necessary to install the printer driver. When you're done, click Next.

   - If you choose to have Windows find and install the driver, Windows 7 will do so and ask you for the name of the printer and whether you want to share this printer with other computers in your HomeGroup. When that process is finished, you'll also be asked to print a test page to make sure the printer is working properly. When you click the Finish button, Windows returns you to the Devices and Printers page.

3. You'll see a screen similar to that shown in Figure 9.12, with icons for the various computers and other devices Windows 7 has detected are connected or available to either your computer or the network to which your computer is connected. Those devices already connected also have a green check mark.

4. If you double-click one of the icons with the green check mark, you'll get a description of the device and its network connection, and you'll be able to see what documents are in queue, whether the device is ready, and other information. If you double-click one of the icons without the green check mark, you'll be able to configure it and connect it to your computer or network.

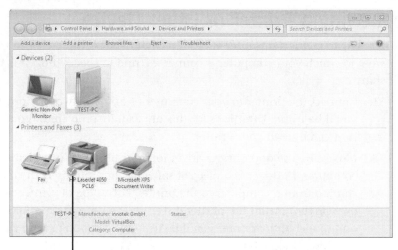

Already connected printers are
displayed with a green check mark

FIGURE 9.12

Connect printers and other devices to your computer or your network.

---

note

You don't have to add USB printer (one that connects directly to your computer via the USB port) because Windows 7 scans for and automatically detects such a printer at startup.

---

5. If you're adding a local printer, you'll be asked which port to use. Most printers use the printer ports in the order shown (LPT1, LPT2, or LPT3). If you're adding another printer to a computer that already has a printer attached, use LPT2 or LPT3. Then click Next.

Uninstalling a Printer

To uninstall a printer (actually, you'll just uninstall the printer driver; you can unplug the printer anytime), click the question mark in the upper-right corner of the page to bring up the Help menu, and type `Uninstall`. Follow the directions that appear, including clicking the appropriate links in the Help material.

Adding a Device Not Shown

If you want to add a device that isn't shown, such as a downloader for pictures taken on your digital camera or cell phone, first connect the device, and then click Add a Device.

Windows searches for connected devices it hasn't yet noted and displays icons corresponding to them. Click the device and follow the instructions for installing any device drivers.

Your HomeGroup

If you are setting up a home network, Windows 7 can make the whole process easier via a new facility called HomeGroup. A HomeGroup is a kind of Windows 7 networking interface which makes it easy to share printers, storage, and media in a home environment.

To set up your HomeGroup

1. Select HomeGroup from the Control Panel.

2. Next, click the Create a HomeGroup button.

3. On the next screen, select what kinds of information you want to share with others at home. See Figure 9.13.

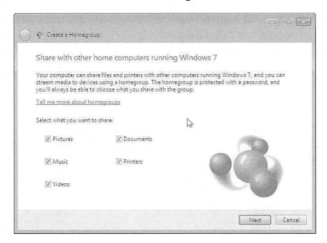

FIGURE 9.13

You can specify which types of files you want to share with others.

4. When done, click the Next button.

5. Windows 7 displays a password screen that will let you share access to other computers. Since this is a temporary password, write it down, including capitalization. You can change it later.

6. Click the Finish button. You have now added your computer to the network called HomeGroup.

> **note**
>
> Note that you can share libraries of files and folders and pictures, music, and videos with other devices (such as wide-screen TV sets in the living room, cell phones, or your children's computers). And note that this sharing is not secure, meaning that anyone connected to your HomeGroup has access to these files.

7. If you want to set up streaming media to other devices, this is the place to do it. Check the Stream My Pictures, Music, and Videos to All Devices on my Home Network box and click the Save Changes button.

    Otherwise, return to the Create a HomeGroup screen by clicking the left arrow in the upper-left corner of the screen.

8. Next, it's important to change the password to one you'll remember. Scroll down to the lower half of the screen and click Change the Password. You'll need to confirm that you want to change the password.

9. The system will ask you for the new password, but will display a suggested password. If you want to use the suggestion, simply click the Next button. Otherwise, enter your own password (minimum eight characters), one you'll remember, and then click the Next button.

> **tip**
>
> Every time a new user is added to your HomeGroup, that user will need to enter the password you've specified. Once you've logged into the HomeGroup, however, you can select View or Print the Homegroup Password to give it to someone else.

A Word about Password Strength

Strong passwords are a combination of letters and numbers that make it difficult for a hacker or an automatic password attacker to guess the right password. How strong your password is depends on its length, complexity, and randomness. It also depends on how well someone else can guess personal details about you, such as the names and birthdates of your children, your previous addresses or phone numbers, or pet names. And finally it depends on whether you write down the password and store the information in a place that could be found by others. Finally, viruses and other forms of malware can log your keystrokes or invite you to enter personal information in a bogus site; your networks can be wiretapped; and dumpster diving means that someone else can go through your trash and find personal data you've discarded.

In personal passwords, the most common number used is 1, and the most common letters are a, e, o, and r.

tip

Adding another computer to your HomeGroup is not quite the same as adding another computer to your Home network. A HomeGroup is more about securely sharing information, such as files, pictures, music, and video. If a printer is connected through a USB connection to your computer, only those who have the password to connect to the HomeGroup will have access to it. A Home network is more about sharing devices, such as printers, scanners, or faxes, or sharing a direct connection to another computer, and doesn't necessarily require knowledge of a password to use these devices.

Changing Your Homegroup Password

At this point, anyone with the right password will be able to access your HomeGroup and share in the use of devices, files, pictures, music, and videos. So the most important thing for you to do is to change the password, unless you feel that the automatically assigned password is one you and your family will easily remember.

To change the password, on the HomeGroup screen click Change the Password. Enter a password you'll remember in the spaces provided and click Save Changes. Now you can discard the automatically assigned password.

Libraries and Public Folders

Broadly defined, a library is a place where you keep information. In the computer world, a library is usually a collection of folders and files. In Windows 7, you can share access to your libraries, folders, and files by configuring what you want to share in the HomeGroup.

In Windows 7, libraries themselves don't store your files or folders—they point to different folders on your hard disk or on an external drive attached to your computer. This means you have easy access to a group of files regardless of where they are stored. For example, some of your music files might be on your hard disk and some may be on a thumb drive, but if they're organized into the Music Library, you can access all of your music files there.

A folder is another place where you keep information, and a public folder on your computer has information that's available to anyone who has access to your computer or has been given permission via your HomeGroup. A personal folder on your computer is accessible only by you, unless you've given explicit permission to another user.

Your computer has both Personal and Public folders in the Documents, Music, Pictures, and Videos libraries. It also stores other public files at C:\Users\Public. Personal user folders are at C:\Users\<username>.

Many of the common user folders have been renamed in Windows 7. Windows Vista had Documents, Downloads, Photos, Videos, and Music. In Windows 7, these folders have been renamed as Personal Documents, Personal Downloads, Personal Photos, Personal Videos, and Personal Music. This lets you more easily distinguish between public and personal documents.

Creating a New Library

Even though Windows 7 comes with a decent selection of built-in libraries, it is likely that you will want to create your own, too. Here's how:

1. Click the Start icon; then click on Computer on the right side of the screen.

2. Scroll through the list of locations on the left side of the screen; then click Libraries.

3. With the Libraries window open, right-click anywhere in the window, and then click New, Library (see Figure 9.14), and give your new library a name. From here on, your new library will be included in the list of Libraries in the navigation pane.

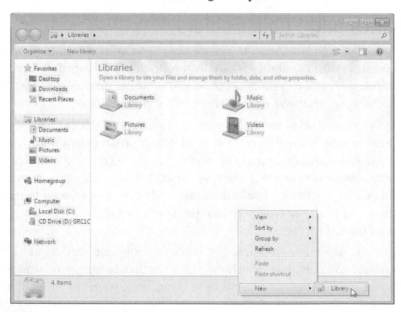

FIGURE 9.14

Windows 7 gives you the ability to create your own libraries.

4. After you create the library, you should decide what you want included. If you have already created a file (document, picture, music, or video), right-click the folder or file and click Properties.

5. On the Library tab, click Add, select a folder, and then click Include in Library. You can include as many folders and files in your library as you want.

Network and Sharing Options

You can change many aspects of how your network is connected and how information is shared from the Network and Sharing Center (see Figure 9.2 earlier in the chapter).

To change the setting by which this network is connected, click Change Adapter Settings. This lets you specify the type of connection this network uses to talk to other computers. If you have an Internet connection set up, it will be one of the options shown. If you have a broadband connection, such as a cable modem, it will also appear. Any other network connections that the system has detected will also be displayed.

To change other network settings, click Change Advanced Sharing Settings. This lets you specify which network settings you want to change. This window displays options you can change for each network to which your computer is connected, with the Home or Work network shown first. Settings you can change include

- Network Discovery, which allows (or disallows) your system to automatically detect what other computers and devices are available for connection to your network

- File and Printer Sharing, which allows (or disallows) you to share access to various files and printers

- Sharing of Public Folders, which allows (or disallows) your public folders to be shared

- Media Streaming, which allows (or disallows) you to stream your music and video files to other devices, such as the living room TV set

- File Sharing Connections, which allow (or disallow) other users to access certain encrypted files

- Sharing of Passwords, which means you can allow (or disallow) specified other users to have password-protected access to your computer

- HomeGroup Connections, which allows (or disallows) the system to use your HomeGroup account and password to connect to all of your computers in your HomeGroup

In each case, you can turn the feature on or off, or in the case of file sharing, specify the type of protection.

Troubleshooting

From the Network and Sharing screen, if you click Troubleshoot a Problem, you will see the window shown in Figure 9.15, asking what you want to fix.

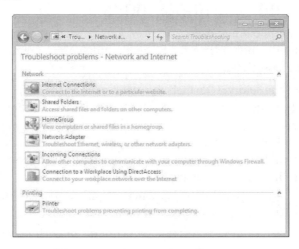

FIGURE 9.15

Troubleshooting a network problem is made a bit easier by built-in troubleshooting tools.

If you select one of the options on this screen, Windows 7 searches for and attempts to fix any network issues. If it can't fix the problem on the first pass, it gives you several other options for fixing the problem yourself.

Using the Windows Media Player

The Windows Media Player is normally connected to your system via settings in your HomeGroup. Turn on Windows Media Player streaming support in the Advanced Sharing Settings window and your computer will detect other WMP libraries on the network and allow playback from them, as well as allowing other computers and devices to be able to read and play the shared media content.

Windows 7 and Domains

With more and more people working from home on laptops or having the option to do so these days, Microsoft's developers decided to include in Windows 7 the capability for these mobile workers to enjoy some of the media content they have on the other PCs in their HomeGroup while they work. At work, instead of a HomeGroup, the laptops are usually joined in domains, which are groups of computers and other devices to which certain permissions are attached.

Those work computers used a specialized domain controller system to manage the permissions. Any computer in the domain would log in to the domain controller, rather than directly into the local system.

Windows HomeGroup brings that centralized permission capability to your home computer. When you create a HomeGroup, you are in essence creating a small, localized domain. One nice feature about this is that joining the HomeGroup doesn't obstruct you from logging in to your work-based domain at the same time. Normally, your computer is only allowed to belong to one domain at a time. HomeGroups allow your computer to belong to a work domain and your HomeGroup simultaneously.

This enables the domain-joined computer to consume the media available on Windows 7 PCs in the home, watch TV through WMC, listen to music via WMP, or print to the printer on another HomeGroup PC. It's done simply by entering the same password you use to connect to your HomeGroup.

The only apparent difference is that protected content on the corporate network is never shared with the HomeGroup computers other than the one that's connected. In essence, the domain-joined computer can see and use the resources on both networks, but nothing else can. Thus, other computers on your work network can't see the resources available through your HomeGroup, and other computers on your HomeGroup can't see the systems on your company network.

10

Windows 7 Wireless Networking

Wireless networks are increasingly common in the network infra-
structures of many companies and organizations. Beyond the office,
roaming users frequently find themselves trying to connect to the
Internet or to the corporate network via wireless networks at coffee
shops, hotels, conference centers, and airports.

Windows 7 makes it easy to see and connect to networks on your
laptop wherever you go. Just click the Network and Sharing Center
icon on the Control Panel.

When you open the Network and Sharing Center, and you click on
Connect to a Network, you see all your wireless and wired options—
Wi-Fi, mobile broadband, dial-up, or corporate virtual private
network (VPN) (see Figure 10.1). The wireless networks appear only
if your computer has a wireless network adapter and driver
installed, the adapter is enabled, and wireless networks are
available.

If you're already connected to
a network, it will show up here.

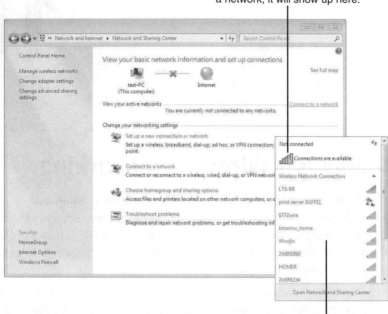

These wireless networks are available,
and you may connect to them
provided the network is open to anyone
or you have the necessary credentials.

FIGURE 10.1

You can see all available wireless networks via the Network and Sharing Center.

Setting Up a Wireless Network

> **note**
>
> Directions in this chapter assume that you have already set up a connection to
> the Internet, as described in Chapter 9. If you haven't already done so, please
> check the directions in Chapter 9 and establish a connection to the Internet.

Getting connected to a wireless network is pretty straightforward. Here's
how:

1. If you haven't already connected to a wireless network via the
    Available Networks dialog, choose Start, Control Panel, Networking
    and Sharing Center, and then choose Set Up a New Connection or
    Network. You can choose from several options:

- If you have a wireless router or network, or if you're within range of a wireless hot spot, click the Connect to the Internet option. You should also click this option if you are using a broadband connection to the outside world.

- If you have a broadband modem (DSL) or a cable modem, and you have a Point-to-Point over Ethernet (PTPoE) account (one that requires a user ID and password to connect), choose the Broadband option.

- If you have a dial-up modem or ISDN, click the Dial-up option.

2. Follow the instructions to log in to your Internet account, including giving this connection a name.

3. If you intend to allow other users of your computer to use this connection, click the permission box.

4. From this point on, your connection to your wireless network can be used, with a few limitations:

   - If this is your in-house network and intended to be used only for connecting multiple computers to the printer, scanner, or other shared devices, you may not be able to get to the Internet on this particular network. If you have plugged your wireless network into some form of outside network connection, such as a broadband connection that's plugged into the wireless network, then you can use the wireless network to connect to that, and thence to the outside world. If, on the other hand, you don't have that outside connection, then you will be unable to use the wireless network

   - If this network is connected via the Internet to a business network, that will be the network you can use.

   - If you're using a coffee shop's wireless connection or possibly a municipal wireless system, you'll be able to browse the Internet.

So, for example, our office has a DSL line, connected to a wireless router. We can use that wireless connection to access the Internet via the DSL line. In addition, Google has implemented a municipal wireless network in the area, so we can also use their wireless network to directly access the Internet.

Viewing and Connecting to Available Wireless Networks

To see what your options are, and to connect to a nearby wireless network, follow these steps:

1. On the Network and Sharing Center window, you will see a list of available networks.

---

tip

If you're used to the way Vista handled network connection, Windows 7 shows fewer network adaptors than Vista. The navigation, sharing, and discovery options have been moved to other sections. The Network and Sharing options in Vista have been moved to the Choose Homegroup and Sharing Options window in Windows 7. The navigation options from Vista have been moved to the Network and Internet option on the Control Panel in Windows 7. To learn more about HomeGroups and sharing, see Chapter 9, "Windows Networking."

---

2. To connect to an existing network, in this case a wireless network, click Connect to a Network, as shown in Figure 10.2.

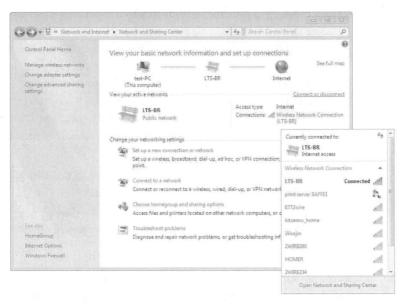

FIGURE 10.2

The Network and Sharing Center shows a list of available networks.

3. On the right of your screen, you'll see the Currently Connected To window, with the list of your current connections.

note

The number of bars shown on the right for each connection shows the strength of the connection. More bars, of course, is better and means a faster connection. Some networks require a network security key or password or phrase. These are indicated by a small yellow icon above the bars on the right. To connect to one of those networks, ask the network administrator or the service provider for the security key or password.

caution

Whenever you can, you should connect only to security-enabled wireless networks. If you connect to a network that's not secure, someone with the right tools may be able to see everything that you do, including the websites you visit, the documents you work on, and the usernames and passwords that you use. Changing your network location to Public can help minimize the risk. For more on network security considerations, see the following section, "How Do I Know if a Wireless Network Is Secure?"

How Do I Know if a Wireless Network Is Secure?

There is no way to guarantee complete security on a wireless network. However, you can take some precautions to help minimize security risks when you use a wireless network.

Whenever possible, connect only to wireless networks that require a network security key or password or have some other form of security, such as a certificate. The information sent over these networks is encrypted, which can help protect your computer from unauthorized access. When you view available wireless networks on the Connect to a Network window, wireless networks that have not enabled security will be identified with a yellow icon (see Figure 10.3).

Before you connect to a network provided by a wireless Internet service provider (ISP), such as a public network in a coffee shop or an airport, read the privacy statement carefully and make sure that you understand which files, if any, are saved to your computer and what type of information the network provider collects from your computer.

Your best guarantee of privacy, however, is to be vigilant about what's allowed to enter your computer. Remember the oft-repeated warnings about not opening email from any source you don't recognize, and be extra careful about responding to any request for personal information, including entering a user ID and password upon logging in. If the yellow icon has appeared for the network you're logging in to, at least you'll know that you are on a public network, and you can take appropriate precautions. Make sure your antispam and anti-malware software is up-to-date when logging on to coffee shop and other public networks.

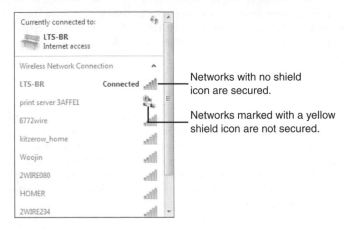

Networks with no shield icon are secured.

Networks marked with a yellow shield icon are not secured.

FIGURE 10.3

The yellow icon clearly identifies wireless networks that are not secure.

What Makes a Home or Work Network Safe to Connect To?

Not all home or work networks are safe. One or more of the other users of your home network may, for instance, have accidentally downloaded a keylogger while playing an online game or downloading some clip art.

To help ensure that a home or work network is safe to connect to, make sure that it has the following:

- For wireless networks, a wireless connection encrypted with Wi-Fi Protected Access (WPA or WPA2). (WPA2 is preferred because it is more secure than WPA.)

- For all networks, a firewall or other device with network address translation (NAT), which is connected between your computer or wireless access point and your cable or DSL modem (see Figure 10.4).

Many modern cable and DSL modems include both NAT and wireless capabilities, built in. Wireless routers, in addition, are also often capable of acting as NAT devices. Our recommendation is that, if you have a broadband connection, you have some form of NAT capability between the modem and your computer—either directly (built in to the cable/DSL modem) or as a standalone device.

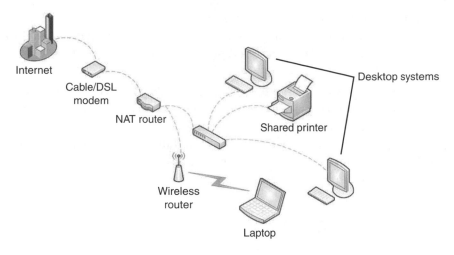

FIGURE 10.4

Make sure that your network has a firewall between your computer or wireless access point and your modem.

In Figure 10.4, you can see an example where the NAT device and the wireless router are separate from the cable/DSL modem,

How Windows Firewall Affects Network Locations

One difference between your home or work networks and a public network is how this affects the protection levels on your computer. At home, or on a work network, you should be able to count on a hardware firewall, such as a NAT router, protecting your computer from prying eyes. When you are on a public network, however, you don't have that option and you are forced to rely on a software firewall to protect your computer.

So, when you are on your home or work networks, you are generally more willing to allow various programs to run and access the Internet. Why? Because you are already protected from unauthorized access.

The public network location blocks certain programs and services from running to help protect your computer from unauthorized access while you're connected to a network in a public place. If you're connected to a public network and Windows Firewall is turned on, some programs or services might ask you to allow them to communicate through the firewall so that they will work properly.

When you allow a program to communicate through the firewall, it's allowed for every network with the same location as the network you're currently connected to. For example, if you connect to a network in a coffee shop and choose Public network as the location and then you unblock an instant message program, that program will be unblocked for all public networks that you connect to.

If you plan to unblock multiple programs while you're connected to a public network, consider changing the network location to home network or work network. It might be safer to change this one network than affect every public network you connect to from that point on. But remember that if you make that change, your computer will be visible to others on the network, and this can be a substantial security risk.

Some Wi-Fi Limitations

When connecting to a Wi-Fi network, your Internet connection speed can be affected by a variety of factors, including where your computer is located, whether other wireless devices are in the same area, and even what the slowest connection is beyond the wireless router. Wireless networks operate on frequencies that are similar to those used by other devices, such as microwave ovens or cordless phones. Operating a 2.4 gigahertz (GHz) cordless phone next to your 2.4GHz wireless laptop can cause interference or completely block the wireless network connection. If you want to make phone calls while surfing the Web, either use a wired telephone or a cordless phone that operates at a different frequency than your wireless network.

One point that many people don't realize is that even if you have a high-speed wireless network connection (the 802.11g protocol, for example, supports up to 54Mbit network connections), you can still be limited by the speed of the connection from that router to the Internet. So if your favorite coffee shop has 54Mbit wireless connection, but uses a 1.5Mbit DSL router to connect out to the Internet, your network connection (and that of everyone else in the coffee shop sharing that connection with you) will be limited to the 1.5Mbit DSL connection.

How close you are to the wireless access point or router, as well as physical obstructions, can affect the quality of your Internet connection. To improve your connection speed, move closer to the access point and make sure that there are no physical obstructions between the access point and your computer.

note

Worth noting is that a "physical obstruction" can be many things. One wireless
access point we use in downtown San Jose, for example, has a tree between
where we work and the actual antenna. During dry weather, the tree isn't much
of an obstacle. When it rains, however, the water collecting on the leaves of the
tree is enough of a physical obstacle to the radio waves that it causes substantial problems.

Choosing a Network Location

The first time that you connect to a network, you must choose a network
location. This automatically sets the appropriate firewall and security settings for the type of network that you connect to. If you connect to networks in different locations (for example, a network at your home, at a
local coffee shop, or at work), choosing a network location can help
ensure that your computer is always set to an appropriate security level.

There are four network locations:

- **Home Network**—Choose Home Network for home networks or when
  you know and trust the people and devices on the network.
  Computers on a home network can belong to a HomeGroup.
  Network discovery is turned on for home networks, which allows you
  to see other computers and devices on the network and allows other
  network users to see your computer.

- **Work Network**—Choose Work Network for small office or other
  workplace networks. Network discovery, which allows you to see
  other computers and devices on a network and allows other network
  users to see your computer, is on by default, but you can't create or
  join a HomeGroup.

- **Public Network**—Choose Public Network for networks in public
  places (such as coffee shops or airports). This location is designed to
  keep your computer from being visible to other computers around
  you and to help protect your computer from any malicious software
  from the Internet. HomeGroups are not available on public networks, and network discovery is turned off. You should also choose
  this option if you're connected directly to the Internet without using
  a router or if you have a mobile broadband connection.

- **Domain Network**—The Domain Network location is used for
  domain networks such as those at enterprise workplaces. This type of
  network location is controlled by your network administrator and

can't be selected or changed. One advantage of Domain Networks is that they allow you to centrally manage resources and permissions for all of your users. If you are using domains, you should refer to your network documentation and check with Microsoft about configuring your Windows 7 systems to properly run on your domain.

note

If you know you won't need to share files or printers, the safest choice is Public Network.

To Change a Network Location

Here's how to change a network location:

1. Open the Network and Sharing Center by clicking the Start button, Control Panel, Network and Sharing Center.

2. Click Work Network, Home Network, or Public Network, and then click the network location you want.

3. Select a network and click Connect or Disconnect (see Figure 10.5).

FIGURE 10.5

Select a network and click Connect.

tip

If you want Windows to automatically connect to a network without any intervention from you, select Connect Automatically as shown in Figure 10.5.

caution

Choosing Home Network or Work Network changes the firewall configuration to allow communication to and from your computer, which can be a security risk.

Connecting to the Internet

The Connect to the Internet Wizard will guide you through the steps of setting up an Internet connection:

1. Open the Connect to the Internet Wizard by clicking the Start button and then clicking Control Panel.

2. Then click Network and Sharing Center.

3. Click Set up a New Connection or Network and then double-click Connect to the Internet.

note

If you're connected to a local area network, you might already be connected to the Internet. To find out, open your web browser and try accessing a website.

11

Virtualization

Virtualization, simply put, is a method whereby more than one virtual computer shares the resources of a single physical system. It is a software environment that acts like a physical computer, executing programs as if it were one. A single physical computer thus can simultaneously act like one or more virtual computers. Virtualization has several benefits:

- It allows you to run more than one computer on your physical computer, as we'll see a little later in this chapter.

- It provides a layer of protection between the system that you do your work on and the underlying computer system that manages the physical resources of your computer.

- It allows you to use a logical method of using the resources of your computer.

Virtual hard disks (VHDs) are part and parcel of virtualization. A VHD is a single computer file that represents the entire contents of a hard disk. As such, while the underlying (physical) computer thinks of it as a single file, the virtual operating system thinks of the VHD as an entire hard disk, containing thousands of files.

Virtualization works best when you are using, or contemplating using, more than one system to perform specific tasks. As such, it is mostly a business-oriented approach to computing, allowing you to move several computers' worth of "system" onto a single set of hardware.

If you are a home user, we generally can't recommend virtualization as anything other than a special-interest topic, something that you probably won't get much out of. If you are a business user, even someone with a small home office, however, virtualization is something you might want to start thinking about.

Virtualization and VHDs are not new to Windows, having been introduced by Microsoft in 2005 as Microsoft Virtual Server. However, until Windows 7, virtualization has not been available out of the box with Microsoft's desktop operating systems, having previously been aimed at users of their server software. In addition, the availability of the new Windows XP Mode virtual 32-bit system (which we discuss below) is completely new to the Windows world as a product offering. If you are concerned about the stability of your Windows XP–specific applications while running under Windows 7, the section on Windows XP Mode, below, is just for you.

Advantages of Virtualization and VHDs

Using virtualization and VHDs has a number of advantages over standard operating system installations:

- **Better resource utilization**—One of the big issues in many companies, large and small, is buying too many computers to perform multiple tasks. Virtualization essentially eliminates this problem because you can buy a single computer and use it to handle multiple requests. Need a separate server for your financials? No problem. How about a separate server for your customer database? Not a problem. Virtualization allows you to create these servers on-the-fly, without having to buy and configure new hardware each time a new request comes up.

- **Speed of deployment**—Creating a new virtual server is a simple task, taking only a few minutes. You can go from "I need a new machine to do this task" to "it's done" in under 10 minutes, including the time to create the virtual server, configure it, load a fully configured template, configure that with specific information such as name and IP, and test it to make sure that it's ready for use. Compare that with having to buy a new PC, configuring the new PC, and getting it up and running. In the time it would take you to unpack your new machine from its boxes, you can have your new virtual server up and running.

- **Lower operating costs**—Frankly, virtual systems are cheaper to run. They require less power and don't take as much effort to cool. Which means that in addition to not having to buy a new machine each time, you don't have to pay as much to run it, either.

- **Upgrades and migration**—Suppose that you have a particular virtual server that is consuming an expanding amount of resources—more RAM, more hard disk space, more everything—and you need to upgrade it. If it were a physical server, you'd have the problem of getting the new machine up, then moving everything cleanly, then shutting down the old server and making sure that the transition went smoothly. With a virtual machine, that problem essentially goes away. Yes, you'll need the new hardware, but by transferring a copy of the virtual server across to the new machine, you can migrate the entire operating environment in just a matter of minutes. You can use the same technique for upgrades. Just shift your VM from one machine to another and then take the old machine offline while you perform your maintenance.

- **Deploying standard systems**—One issue we've always considered a real nuisance is deploying a "standard" system image when we bring up a new computer. First you have to load the operating system. Then you have to catch up all the system patches. Next you have to run the entire checklist of "is this software loaded," and configure it for your company, and make sure that is all up-to-date and patched. It can take hours. With VHDs, this becomes incredibly easy. After you've created a template system, all you have to do is copy the VHD for the template to some form of storage, such as a DVD, a thumb drive, or a network drive. The next time you need to load a system, you can bypass the bulk of your problem by loading the VHD directly to the disk and launching it.

note

To illustrate how system images work, we used this feature while we were developing this chapter, testing on one machine, creating on another, and shooting the artwork on a third, all using the same set of virtual machine files.

- **Backups**—Another aspect of virtualization that we've found to be tremendously useful is in backing up systems after they're configured. Because the entire operating system image is a single file, it's quite simple to store a version of that entire file elsewhere, for easy recovery. This is useful in a number of ways. First, it lets you keep a complete snapshot of a system—for example, your desktop. Second, it's also useful when you have to set up and tear down systems on a regular basis—such as when you need a test environment or if you need environments for a training class.

Disadvantages of Virtualization and VHDs

There are, however, some disadvantages to virtualization:

- **Some apps require a dedicated PC**—Some applications still require dedicated physical resources. Take, for example, a rendering machine for a small graphics shop. Rendering is a process where processing time is highly dependent on the amount of available RAM and CPU. So although you can create multiple virtual rendering servers, they're still working from the same pool of available resources, meaning that there's no net benefit—and in fact, virtualization would be a bad idea because each virtual server consumes some of those resources as well, leaving fewer resources for the actual work at hand.

- **Licensing fees**—Watch out for licensing fees. IT professionals call this "license creep." If you let the number of virtual servers get out of hand, you may find that you're paying a lot more money than you should in licensing fees. So pay attention to how your software licenses are structured.

- **Better for server processes than desktops**—Be aware that virtualization is really most useful when dealing with server processes; it can be less useful for dedicated desktops.

Virtualization and VHDs in Action

Following are a few real-world examples of people we know who use virtualization, to illustrate why it might be useful—and where it stops being such a great idea.

As you will see, virtualization is not for everyone, or for every situation. In many home situations, virtualization doesn't provide much benefit, even while it adds to the complexity of your system. If, however, you are a power user who needs the equivalent of several systems to do all your work, you might find that virtualization has some significant benefits. Office users also might benefit from virtualization, both in terms of enhanced system security and for the ease with which the system environment can be deployed.

Example 1: Garage-Based Manufacturer

The first example is a manufacturer we know who builds small, specialized equipment for performance cars (we're going to refer to them simply as widgets) out of a facility in his garage. He deals with an extensive client base around the world, taking orders by mail order, by fax, and over the Internet, and he keeps himself and his two employees busy. His order entry/accounting system, though, runs on a total of three computers: One houses his order-entry database; a second one houses his accounting and shipment-processing software; and the third is his working desktop, where he reads the incoming email orders, runs spreadsheet calculations, and so on.

Our friend the widget manufacturer wants to modernize a bit and get rid of the multiple switches, monitors, and keyboards that he has to keep track of every time he changes systems to perform another step in his order-delivery process. He is an excellent candidate for virtualization because he could virtualize both his accounting database and his order-entry database, putting each in a separate virtual computer living on his high-performance desktop system. Given the upgraded inventory database he's looking at investing in, virtualization might be a good idea.

Example 2: Freelance Graphic Artist and Publisher

The second example is a freelance graphic artist, photographer, and small-press publisher. She works from her home, working around her two daughters. During her downtime, she lets the girls use the office computer for games and schoolwork.

Because she wears multiple hats, and they're all "small business" hats, our friend the publisher needs more than one system. She needs a high-performance graphic arts/publishing system, an "office" desktop—and she'd like to have a separate system for the kids to do their work on that protects her work environment from being infected by viruses or running into problems from games.

For her purposes, virtualization is almost ideal. She can configure a common "basic" desktop and then set up separate virtual systems for her graphic arts work, for her office needs, and for the kids. This keeps any security risks to a minimum and provides an easy method of backing up her artwork and production environment—she can simply back up the appropriate virtual system. It also provides a nearly impenetrable way to isolate the effects of her kids' web surfing from her office and work environments.

Example 3: Multiple Home Users Under the Same Roof

One older family friend has several people using his computer. Each uses it for different things. He uses the computer for web surfing, email, and doing taxes. Someone else uses it for light office work, and the guest account uses it for web access.

In this case, there really isn't any point in using virtualization. Separate user accounts provide all the access control needed, and there isn't a significant gain to be had from providing separate system environments.

Using Windows 7 Virtualization

Windows 7 includes a number of new virtualization features that have not previously been available in the desktop version of Windows—and in fact have only recently been available in the Server editions aimed at large corporate data centers. The two primary features in this are Virtual Hard Disks, used in creating virtual systems, and the new Windows XP virtualization feature, called *Windows XP Mode*.

Virtual Hard Disks

A VHD is a single file that contains the complete contents and structure that represents a hard disk drive. VHDs are frequently used to store multiple copies of operating systems, their associated programs, and even local copies of data in a single file that can be used by various virtualization programs. A VHD lets you move back and forth between operating systems, depending on the environment in which you want to run.

Virtual hard disks are different from logical hard disks, which you may have run into in the past. A logical hard disk is a single physical hard disk that has been divided into two or more "logical" drives, each of which is assigned its own drive letter. You might do this when you have a single big drive and want to keep the contents of the logical drives separate, such as when you're sharing the contents to a group of users over a network or if you want to keep one logical drive (the C: drive) for the operating system and applications, and another (the D: drive, in this example) for your working files. Properly speaking, you *always* have a logical drive on your hard disk—usually, the physical drive is configured with just one logical drive (the C: drive) so you don't see it split in two.

A virtual hard disk, in contrast, resides on the same logical drive as any other file. It is, however, a big file that contains an image of the contents of an entire hard disk, including the operating system. Because it is a single file, you can do a number of things easily with the virtual hard disk that would be much more difficult to do with, for instance, a logical hard disk.

Virtual hard disks are an easy way to deploy virtual versions of a system.

After you have created a single instance of a VHD, you can copy that file, easily duplicating your virtual computer system. Because the information is still stored in a single file, you can also easily back up the entire system image by copying the entire file to a safe location.

The VHD Image file format is currently supported by a number of virtualization software packages, including the following:

- Microsoft Windows Hyper-V (on Windows Server 2008)
- Sun Microsystems VirtualBox
- VMWare ESX Server
- Citrix XenServer Hypervisor
- Microsoft Windows 7

Native Hard Disk Support in Windows 7

Windows 7 provides a unique capability, in that you can create, mount, and boot from a VHD file directly from the operating system, rather than requiring a software overlay, such as VirtualBox or ESX Server.

What this means is this: When dealing with most virtualization solutions, such as VirtualBox or VMWare, you need to install an underlying operating system (which controls the physical assets of your computer), then add in the virtualization software (VirtualBox, or the appropriate VMWare software), and then create and run a virtual Windows 7 system inside that. Think of it as a three-layer cake:

The bottom layer is the underlying operating system.

The middle layer is the virtualization software, which manages the VHD.

The top layer is your Windows 7 system.

Microsoft's native hard disk support for VHDs allows you to dispense with running a software overlay, such as the aforementioned VirtualBox or ESX Server. In this new model, your Windows 7 system manages its own virtualization, so there is no need for an underlying operating system and no separate virtualization software—all three layers of the cake are collapsed back into one layer.

So how do you create a VHD and install Windows 7 to it?

Creating a VHD

The simplest method is to use the Windows 7 installation DVD to create the VHD and then install Windows 7 into that VHD. Follow these steps:

1. Boot your system using the Windows 7 DVD.
2. Choose Repair Your Computer as shown in Figure 11.1.

FIGURE 11.1

To create a VHD and install Windows 7 on it, choose Repair Your Computer.

3. Click Next without selecting a particular destination.
4. Select Command Prompt (see Figure 11.2).

FIGURE 11.2

Choose the Command Prompt.

5. Type **diskpart** and press Enter to start the Diskpart utility.

6. Type `create vdisk file="c:\Windows7Build.vhd" type=expandable maximum=40000` and press Enter, as shown in Figure 11.3.

---

tip

You can create any VHD filename you want, as long as there are no spaces in the filename. Note that the *maximum* parameter is the maximum size of the virtual hard disk in megabytes. You can make it larger if that is appropriate.

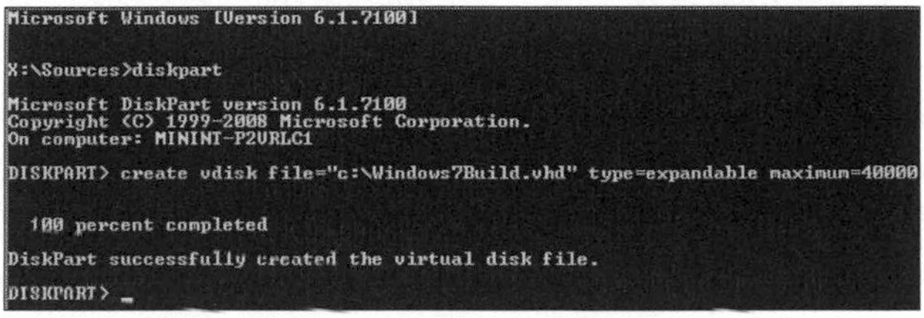

FIGURE 11.3

Name your VHD.

7. Type `select vdisk file="c:\Windows7Build.vhd"` and press Enter.

8. Type `attach vdisk` and press Enter.

9. Type `exit` and press Enter to quit Windows Repair. DO NOT REBOOT. Instead, click the [X] at the top right corner to close the Windows Repair window, and return to the installer.

10. Next, you create a partition in the new hard disk that you have just created. Start by clicking Install Now. When the License terms window appears, click "I accept the license terms"; then click the Next button.

11. Now click the option to install a new copy of Windows. You will be asked where you want to install the new copy of Windows. Choose the partition containing the virtual hard disk you just created.

12. Format the new hard disk partition by selecting the partition and then clicking the Next button. This also starts the installation process.

13. Install Windows 7 to this new hard disk. See Chapters 3 and 4 for specific instructions on installing Windows 7. Figure 11.4 shows the Windows 7 installation in progress.

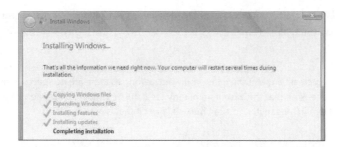

FIGURE 11.4

Installing Windows 7 could take a while, so use this opportunity to take a coffee break.

14. Reboot to launch Windows 7.

15. After your Windows 7 installation is running the way you want, back up the VHD file. This provides a clean image of your system that can then be readily reloaded to your computer if needed.

> **note**
>
> We've also found a number of other methods for creating VHDs and installing Windows 7 documented online by Windows developers around the world. Most of these are variations on creating a Windows system image (a WIM file) and converting it to a VHD, most often using the WIM2VHD utility available at http://code.msdn.microsoft.com/wim2vhd. We found literally thousands of results when we searched on the terms "Windows 7 create VHD."

Dependent VHDs

You can also create dependent VHDs—multiple VHDs that depend on a parent VHD. Why would this be useful? Suppose you have 10 employees, but they basically use three configurations:

- Office admin configuration
- Graphics configuration
- Developer configuration

With a dependent VHD approach, you could create one parent VHD (the common company configuration, which might have your company-standard email/web software, antivirus software, network configuration, user accounts, and so forth). Then you could create the three dependent VHDs, one for each configuration:

- Office admin VHD, containing finance software

- Graphics VHD, containing graphic editing software
- Developer VHD, containing a complete programming environment

You could then distribute these VHDs to company employees as appropriate, standardizing software usage across your company with no trouble.

To create dependent VHDs, you'll need to follow the steps outlined in the section "Creating a VHD" earlier in this chapter, but add one additional parameter when you create the VHD. In step 6, add the parameter

```
parent="c:\Windows7base.vhd"
```

Then complete the rest of the steps as described.

Creating VHDs from Within Windows 7

After you have installed Windows 7, it is quite simple to create VHDs.

1. From the Control Panel, select "System and Security" and then "Administrative Tools".

2. Select the Computer Management option.

3. In the left pane, select Storage, Disk Management.

4. From the Action menu, select Create VHD as shown in Figure 11.5.

FIGURE 11.5

Creating VHDs is much simpler after Windows 7 is installed.

Mounting VHDs

As we noted previously, it is possible to mount a VHD at any time using the command line. Follow these steps:

1. Type **diskpart** and press Enter to start the diskpart utility.

2. Type **select vdisk file="c:\Windows7Build.vhd"** and press Enter.

3. Type **attach vdisk** and press Enter (see Figure 11.6).

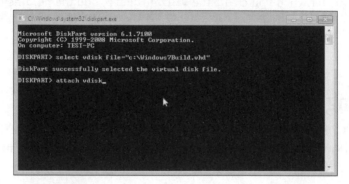

FIGURE 11.6

Mounting a virtual hard disk.

4. Type **exit**.

You can also use the graphic tools within an installed copy of Windows 7 to mount a VHD. Here's how:

1. Select the Computer Management tab.

2. In the left pane, select Storage, Disk Management.

3. From the Action menu, select Attach VHD (see Figure 11.7).

FIGURE 11.7

Choosing the location for your VHD.

Windows XP Mode

Windows XP Mode is a special feature available only on higher-end versions of Windows 7—specifically the Professional, Enterprise, and Ultimate editions (see Figure 11.8). Windows XP Mode provides a fully licensed copy of Windows XP (with Service Pack 3 already installed) running virtually within your Windows 7 system.

Unlike most virtualization solutions, this one does not require that you run the Windows XP instance as a separate desktop. Instead, as you install applications within the virtual XP environment, they are published to the host (Windows 7) operating system as well. Shortcuts for these applications are even placed into the Start Menu. The result? You can run Windows XP–based applications alongside Windows 7 applications on a single desktop.

What's the point of Windows XP Mode? One of the problems that is a continuing concern among many businesses is the stability with which Windows 7 will run applications that were written for Windows XP. This doesn't apply only to custom applications, either—older software of all types has been found to have issues of this sort, even including older versions of Microsoft Office.

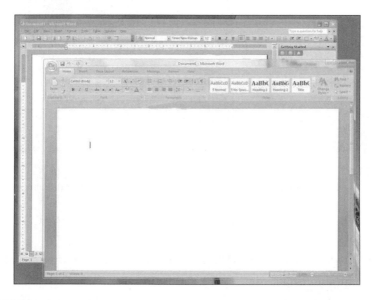

FIGURE 11.8

The Windows XP Mode Desktop.

Windows XP Mode isn't shipped as part of the standard Windows 7 installation DVD. Instead, you download the installation from the Microsoft website (similar to how Live Essentials is handled).

To install Windows XP mode, you need to download two installers—the Windows Virtual PC installer and the Windows XP Mode software, which uses Virtual PC to run. However, before you do this, you should check your machine to make sure it is capable of running Virtual PC, and thus Windows XP Mode.

The reason for this is that Microsoft Virtual PC requires hardware virtualization support, which is only available in newer systems. The best resource we found for determining if your system includes virtualization support was to first find out what kind of processor you have.

How do you do this? Inside Windows 7, open the Control Panel, click System and Security then click System. See Figure 11.9.

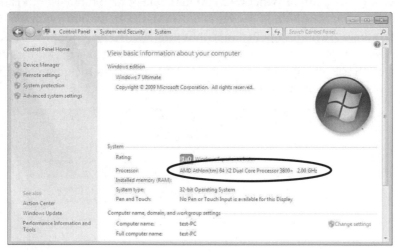

FIGURE 11.9

Open the System Control Panel applet to determine what CPU your computer has installed.

Next, depending on whether your PC uses an Intel or AMD CPU, go to one of these two sites:

- If you have an Intel CPU in your system, point your browser here:

  http://en.wikipedia.org/wiki/X86_virtualization

  Click on the Intel Virtualization technology link. Alternately, you can use the Microsoft Intel Processor Identification Utility, which can be downloaded here:

  http://www.intel.com/support/processors/tools/piu/

- If you have an AMD CPU in your system, point your browser here:

  http://en.wikipedia.org/wiki/List_of_AMD_Athlon_64_microprocessors

  Click the Dual-Core Desktop Processors link, and look for your specific processor. Note that it must be on a list that indicates support for AMD-V. Alternately, you can download the AMD Virtualization Compatibility Check Utility, located here:

  http://support.amd.com/us/Pages/
  dynamicDetails.aspx?ListID=c5cd2c08-1432-4756-
  aafa-4d9dc646342f&ItemID=172

Once you have verified that your PC uses a CPU capable of using viralization, you can get started with installing Windows XP Mode. Here's how:

1. Go to http://www.microsoft.com/windows/virtual-pc/download.aspx and download the Windows Virtual PC and Windows XP Mode installers. Note that this link also includes instructions on how to enable hardware virtualization on your PC, if your computer's CPU supports hardware virtualization.

2. Install Windows Virtual PC. Your system needs to be rebooted after you have installed Virtual PC.

3. After you have restarted your system, and Virtual PC has completed its installation, install Windows XP Mode (see Figure 11.10).

FIGURE 11.10

The Windows XP mode installer.

4. Accept the Virtual Windows XP license.

5. Set up the user and password for the virtual Windows XP system, as shown in Figure 11.11.

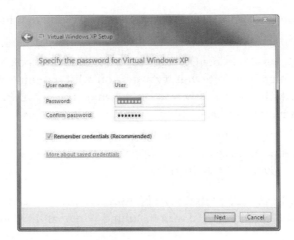

FIGURE 11.11

Choose a password.

6. Finish the setup as you would for a regular Windows XP installation.

7. Start the virtual system.

8. After you've started the virtual Windows XP system, you'll see what looks like a standard Windows XP desktop (see Figure 11.12). The only difference is that it will have a new menu bar at the top, which controls the virtual shell that the Windows XP instance runs in.

FIGURE 11.12

Starting the virtual system.

Configuring Windows XP Mode

After you've installed the virtual Windows XP system, you need to configure it and then install software:

1. From the Tools menu in the virtual machine, select Settings. This allows you to configure a variety of system settings that apply to the virtual machine.

2. The first thing that you will do when you start Windows XP Mode is to set the password used by Virtual Windows XP. Enter the password, and a confirmation of that password, before clicking the Next button.

3. Next, you will be asked to configure the update policy for the virtual Windows XP subsystem. Because this is a fully functional Windows XP Pro installation, it will have the same network vulnerabilities that a standalone Windows XP system would.

tip

Because the virtual Windows XP system is fully licensed, we suggest you turn on Automatic Updates, unless there is a good reason not to, and you are fully aware of the consequences of that choice.

4. Once you've completed these steps, the virtual Windows XP system will start up for the first time. The system will "set itself up" just like it would for a regular installation. It will also enable the integration features that allow Windows XP Mode to tie into Windows 7.

Virtual Windows XP Menus

The system window that Virtual Windows XP opens on your desktop has several menus across the top, allowing you to configure the virtual system as needed.

Action Menu

Table 11.1 explains the available options.

Table 11.1—Action Menu

View Full Screen	This item expands the virtual Windows XP system window to the full size of your screen.
Sleep	Puts the virtual Windows XP system to sleep. Does NOT put your Windows 7 system to sleep, however.
Restart	Restarts and reloads the virtual Windows XP system.
Close	Quits the virtual Windows XP system and closes Windows Virtual PC. Does not exit Windows 7.

USB Menu

This menu lists all USB devices that Windows has identified and gives you the option of attaching/detaching and sharing/not sharing each device.

Tools Menu

This menu has two options as shown in Table 11.2.

Table 11.2—Tools Menu

Disable integration features	This item turns off the Windows XP integration with Windows 7 and runs the virtual Windows XP system as a separate, discrete virtual system. If you have previously disabled integration, reselecting this item will turn the integration features back on.
Settings	Brings up the Virtual PC settings dialog box. This dialog shows the various system settings configured for your virtual Windows XP system. If you have shut down the virtual Windows XP system, but have the Virtual PC window up, you can modify these settings. Note that this is only possible if the virtual Windows XP system is not running.

Why Use Windows XP Mode?

One of the more useful features of Windows XP Mode is that, because it is still a fully featured installation of Windows XP, it can be controlled in the same manner as a standard desktop installation of Windows XP. This becomes important if you are using server-based policy tools, such as Active Directory and Group Policy.

In addition, Windows XP Mode gives you complete protection in terms of application compatibility by providing 100% compatibility with an application that already runs on Windows XP.

The whole point of this exercise is ultimately to make sure that you can always run your applications in some form of a Windows 7 environment, whether that's natively on the Windows 7 desktop or virtually by way of Windows XP Mode.

Windows 7 and Existing Virtualization Environments

So far we have only discussed the virtualization capabilities inherent in Windows 7—virtually loading Windows 7 and using the Windows XP Mode virtual system within Windows 7.

Windows 7 can also be deployed into other virtual environments, however, and the remainder of this chapter discusses our experience in doing so. If you are interested in virtualizing Windows 7 under another virtual environment, we strongly suggest you get thoroughly acquainted with the specific virtual environment that you are considering moving to.

Sun xVM VirtualBox

The first environment we want to discuss is Sun's xVM VirtualBox software. This open source virtualization software can be downloaded from www.virtualbox.org and installed on your system. At present, VirtualBox requires one of the following host operating systems to run properly:

- Linux (We have tested this on both Fedora and Ubuntu and have seen no issues.)
- Mac OS X
- OS/2 Warp
- Windows XP or later
- Solaris

If you plan to run Windows 7 using VirtualBox, you should make sure that your system has sufficient resources for all the various system configurations you plan to use. In addition, allow for system resource utilization by the host and allow 256MB of memory for the VirtualBox software itself. Your video output should also be fully supported by the host system.

Installing Windows 7 Under Sun VirtualBox

Before installing Windows 7 as a virtual system, you need to make sure your host operating system is installed on your computer and you have installed the Sun VirtualBox software.

After you have done these two things, you can start installing Windows 7.

1. Your first task is to start the VirtualBox console and then use it to create and configure a virtual hard disk instance for your Windows 7 installation. We have found that the settings shown in Tables 11.3 and 11.4 are the bare minimum that is acceptable for running Windows 7 from within VirtualBox.

Table 11.3   Minimum Settings for Running Windows 7 Under Sun VirtualBox

OS Type	Microsoft Windows
Version	Windows Vista (see note below)
Base Memory Size	512MB
Boot Hard Disk	Click New, and see below
Hard Disk, Storage Type	Dynamically Expanding Storage
Hard Disk, Location	Any appropriate location on your system
Hard Disk, Size	20.00GB

Table 11.4   Expanded Recommended VirtualBox Settings for Windows 7 Virtual System

Section	Tab	Field	Notes/Entry
General	Basic	Operating System	Microsoft Windows.
	Basic	Version	Windows Vista (we expect that an updated version with Windows 7 compatibility will be available by the end of 2009).
	Basic	Base Memory	800MB.
	Basic	Video Memory	128MB.
	Basic	Enable 3D Acceleration	Yes.
	Advanced	Boot Order	Whatever you think is appropriate. However, note that initially you will need to enable CD/DVD-ROM boot ahead of the hard disk.
	Advanced	Enable ACPI	Yes.
Hard Disk		Enable SATA Controller	Yes.
	Slot	Hard Disk	The VDI file that you create for the virtual system instance.
CD/DVD-ROM		Mount CD/DVD Drive	Yes.
	Host CD/ DVD Drive		Normally we would suggest this. However, see the next item for an alternative option.
	Host CD/ DVD Drive	Enable Passthrough	You *must* enable this option if you plan to let the virtual installation of Windows 7 use your computer's CD/DVD drive.
	ISO Image File		We found some issues with DVD drive passthrough from our host system. As a result, we wound up creating an ISO from the DVD drive on the host system and then mounting the ISO as a DVD image with this option to install Windows 7 to our virtual environment.
Floppy	Mount Floppy Drive		If your system has a floppy drive, and you plan to allow the virtual system to use it, you must

Table 11.4   *Continued*

Section	Tab	Field	Notes/Entry
			select this option. We never used it because none of our test systems had floppy drives.
Audio	Enable Audio		If you want your virtual system to be able to use the host computer's audio capabilities, you must enable this option.
Audio		Host Audio Driver	If you select Null audio driver, the Windows 7 virtual system will "see" an audio card but will not be able to send any sound out through it.
Audio		Audio Controller	SoundBlaster 16.
Network	Adapter 1	Enable Network Adapter	You *must* enable at least one network adapter for your virtual system to be able to communicate on the Internet.
Network	Adapter 1	Adapter Type	Intel Pro/1000 MT Desktop.
Network	Adapter 1	Attached to	NAT.
Network	Adapter 1	Cable Connected	Yes.
Serial Ports	Port 1	Enable Serial Port	Enable this only if you plan to let the virtual system use your computer's serial ports. In our test cases, we left this turned off.
USB		Enable USB Controller	Yes.
USB		Enable USB 2.0 (EHCI) Controller	Yes.
Shared Folder			By default, no shared folders are created. We found it useful to create a shared folder for the virtual system, which linked to the host system's desktop. Click the plus sign (+) icon in the upper-left corner to create a shared folder.

2. After you have created the virtual system instance, including its associated virtual hard disk image (VDI file), you can install Windows 7.

3. Mount the Windows 7 DVD in your system's DVD drive.

4. From within VirtualBox, select the Windows 7 virtual system instance and then click the Start arrow (see Figure 11.13).

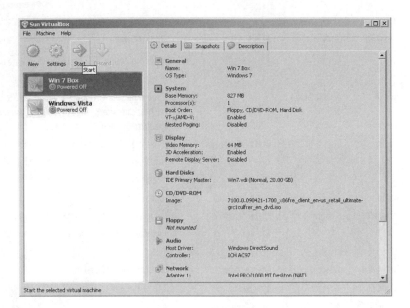

FIGURE 11.13

Starting the Windows 7 instance for system installation.

5. Based on the recommended settings, your virtual system should start to boot and then load from your host system DVD drive. If you have any issues with this process, stop the virtual system, copy an ISO image of the Windows 7 DVD to your system, and then mount that ISO image as the DVD drive under VirtualBox.

6. Install and configure Windows 7 as you normally would.

7. After Windows 7 is installed in your virtual environment, test the network connectivity from within the virtual system using Internet Explorer.

8. Configure the Windows 7 virtual instance as you would any other system installation. Note that you can perform normal application migration operations from within VirtualBox with no issues, so migrating applications and settings should be as simple as they would be to a regular Windows 7 installation.

VMWare

The next environment we discuss is VMWare. In this case, we ran Windows 7 under VMWare Workstation 6.5.2. However, any VMWare product will support the 32-bit x86 platform that you need to run

Windows 7, and virtually any VMWare product that you can get will also support 64-bit Windows 7 installations if your underlying hardware will support it. In practice, this means that you can run Windows 7 virtually under VMWare installed on Windows XP, Vista, Server 2003, Server 2008, any recent version of Linux, and Macintosh OS. The precise operating system requirements may vary depending on which version of VMWare you are using. VMWare Server, for example, requires that you use a server version of Windows as your host operating system; Windows XP and Windows Vista would not work properly.

> **note**
>
> To run the 64-bit version of Windows 7 as a virtual system under VMWare, your host system must have a 64-bit processor and a BIOS compatible with x86 virtualization. Intel systems require VT hardware virtualization, and AMD64 processors must be revision D or later. Also, see the discussion earlier in this chapter about hardware virtualization requirements under Windows XP Mode.

You should note the minimum system requirements for running Windows 7 under VMWare shown in Table 11.5.

Table 11.5 Minimum Requirements to Run Windows 7 Under VMWare

Memory	512MB for VMWare, plus 768MB for Windows 7, totaling 1280MB. Of course, more is better, and VMWare recommends 2GB–4GB of memory to run a guest OS under VMWare.
Disk	VMWare requires 1.7GB for installation purposes. You will also want 20GB of disk space available for the actual Windows 7 installation.

Installing and Configuring VMWare

The first task you need to perform is to install the VMWare software. Install and configure the VMWare environment using the procedures laid out in the VMWare documentation. In our case, we needed to install both VMWare Workstation (which creates the virtual machine) and VMWare Player (which runs it).

After you have done so, create a new virtual machine. During the configuration, you will be asked for the location of the installation media, as well as configuration information, such as your license key and the default user. By entering this information ahead of time, you can allow VMWare to automatically configure the system. This situation also pointed up the ease of having an ISO image of the Windows 7 installer. From within VMWare Workstation, we selected File, New, Virtual Machine, which launched the New Virtual Machine wizard. From there, we selected a typical installation and then pointed the installer at the ISO file we had created earlier. The wizard asked us for a product key, user name, and password; then it asked for a virtual machine name and a location in which to store the virtual machine. Finally, it asked for some configuration information—how big the disk was to be and whether to store the virtual system disk as a single file or split into smaller files.

Once the virtual system was created, we ran it from VMWare Player. The first time we powered up the virtual machine, it automatically detected the ISO; started it; and ran the installation process, configuring the Windows installation using the information we had already entered.

> **note**
>
> One item we noted during our testing process was that configuring VMWare under a Linux host was less simple than configuring other virtual environments. After we got past the configuration issues, however, there were no problems of any kind running Windows 7 under VMWare.

Other Virtual Environments

A number of other virtual environments exist that you can use to virtually deploy Windows 7. As a rule, you should stick to virtualization software that supports either x86 (32-bit) or x64 (64-bit) technologies. Wikipedia maintains a useful list of virtualization software that supports Windows-oriented virtualization.

Moving to a Virtualized Environment

After you make the decision to move to a virtualized environment, most of what you need to do is essentially identical to the standard migration tasks that you'll need to perform for any system migration. System installation, application migration, user configuration setup—all these tasks are identical under virtual environment to what you would normally do for a nonvirtual environment.

The biggest benefit comes when you get to deploying more than one instance of the same virtualized environment. Using the "create once, run many" concept, you can create a standard virtual machine, configure it, and copy the ready-to-go virtual machine definition to every desk that needs it. As an alternative, if you are going to use more than one VM instance on a single system, you can create a common "base" instance and then alter it as needed for each environment you are running.

Index

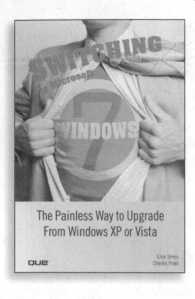

FREE Online Edition

The Painless Way to Upgrade
From Windows XP or Vista

Your purchase of **Switching to Microsoft Windows 7** includes access to a free online edition for 45 days through the Safari Books Online subscription service. Nearly every Que book is available online through Safari Books Online, along with more than 5,000 other technical books and videos from publishers such as Addison-Wesley Professional, Cisco Press, Exam Cram, IBM Press, O'Reilly, Prentice Hall, and Sams.

SAFARI BOOKS ONLINE allows you to search for a specific answer, cut and paste code, download chapters, and stay current with emerging technologies.

Activate your FREE Online Edition at
www.informit.com/safarifree

> **STEP 1:** Enter the coupon code: LWLWXFA.

> **STEP 2:** New Safari users, complete the brief registration form.
> Safari subscribers, just log in.

If you have difficulty registering on Safari or accessing the online edition, please e-mail customer-service@safaribooksonline.com